ISTANBUL

Archaeologist
İlhan Akşit

Gene — Forgive the Gramer
This book was written in
Turkey

(signature)

akşit

AKŞİT KÜLTÜR ve TURİZM TİCARET LTD. ŞTİ.

Contents

Published and distributed by:
AKŞİT KÜLTÜR TURİZM SANAT AJANS
LİMİTED ŞİRKETİ

Cağaloğlu Yokuşu Cemal Nadir Sokak
Nur İş Hanı 2/4   34440 Cağaloğlu
İSTANBUL - TURKEY
Tel: (0-212) 511 53 85 - 527 68 13

Text by	:	İlhan Akşit
Translation	:	Robert Bragner
Photographs	:	Tahsin Aydoğmuş
	:	İzzet Keribar
	:	Yılmaz Dinç
	:	Güngör Özsoy
Graphics by	:	Gülten Aksu
Colour Separation	:	Figür Grafik
Printed By	:	SEÇİL OFSET

THE HISTORY OF ISTANBUL

This is the city that gradually spreads on both sides of the beautiful Bosphorus which was naturally formed early in the IVth Period of Geology as the sea water occupied the deep and narrow valley. The city has been the capital for three empires and been attractive for its historical treasure besides the beauty of the surrounding landscape. In 660 B.C., the Megarians who were leaded by Byzas for settlement in where today Topkapı Palace stands erect, named the city as Byzantion in memory of their commander. However the expeditions indicate older districts of settled-life from 5000 B.C. around Fikirtepe, Kurbağalıdere, Pendik and at Yarımburgaz Cave on the Anatolian side of the Bosphorus.

When the Byzas, Megarians asked their prophets where to set up their "home", their prophets said "against the land of the blinds". On exploration of the Bosphorus the Megarians were fascinated by the uninhabited beauty of the landscape and as the land accross the water was already occupied by the Khalkhedonians, they thought one who leaves such beauty uninhabited and lives against it must be blind and obeyed their prophets' foresight with pleasure.

A century later than the establishment Byzantion was occupied by Persians in 513 B.C. and then by Athens and Spartians. In a period of conflict between Athens and Spartians, Macedonian Kingdom under King Philippos II's reign had become powerful day after day. Although this expansive Kingdom captured Byzantion in 340 B.C., was unable to occupy. After Greece was dominated by Alexander who took over King Philippos II, Persians were also attacked by him and Alexander got hold of Anatolia defeating the Persians in 334 B.C.. Following the death of Alexander, the city was governed by his victorious commanders until it was tremendously destroyed by the Galatian attacks after 278 B.C. In that period of fluctuation, Byzantion eventually was dominated by Romans who were about to establish a global Empire after the defeat of Macedonians in 146 B.C. and the city was governed under the force of Roman State of Thrace. Roman Emperor Septimus Severus ordered total destruction of the Byzantion and massacre of the Byzantians who were with his rival Roman General Niger. As Septimus Severus would not easily give away such a strategical city, later had it rebuilt and changed the name of the city as Antoneinia. The walls surrounding

Christ Mosaics in Chora Monastery.
The mosaic of Emperor Constantin IX. St. Sophia.

the city were expanded, the square in front of St. Sophia Church was reorganised and the road was connected from there to Çemberlitaş. In 203 B.C., construction of a Hippodrome was started and an amphitheatre was built downhill Acropolis nearby Haliç.

Following the defeat of his rival Licinius in 324 A.D, Emperor Constantinus (306-337) started the foundation and development of the city. Initially the Roman Capital was thought to be settled in Troy in memory of mythological Trojan Aeneas however then Byzantion was preferred. The surrounding walls built by Severus, were rebuilt further away in 2.8 km west. The "Forums" (Squares) were connected each other by roads within the walls. Christian

Constantinus had old Pagan temples repaired besides having built the magnificent St. Sophia Church. The restored city was named as Nea Rome and declared to be Capital in 11th May 330 with a tremendous ceremony. Following the death of Constantinus, the name of the city was converted into Constantinopolis. Later on, the name started to be pronounced as Stinpolis, Stinpol, Estanbul and eventually Istanbul.

The competition between Constantinopolis as center of Christianity and Rome as center of Paganism outraged and Constantinopolis became outstanding for Christianity. Theodosius I as a dedicated Orthodox, suppressed the Pagans and in that period of turbulence divided the

View of the Bosphorus, which links Asia and Europe.

Empire into two in 395 A.D. That discrimination ended up with Western Rome, the capital of which was Rome, and Eastern Rome, the capital of which was Constantinopolis. Getting advantage of this division, Western Goths forced the walls of Constantinopolis.

Eastern Roman Empire solved the problem by appointing Alarik the king of Goths as General Commander of the Balcans while Rome, the Capital of Western Roman Empire, was destroyed to a great extent as they failed to perform such a policy (400 A.D). Having survived the occupation of Goths, the Capital of Eastern Roman Empire, Constantinopolis, faced attacks from Huns (440) and could survive only after the dispersion of Hun Empire following the death of Emperor Attila. During this period under stress, the economy failed in Eastern Roman Empire, there arouse deep conflicts between Ariusism and Orthodoxes and even the efforts of Theodosius II's were not enough to solve the problem.

This was when the Haliç and Marmara walls were built inside the outer surrounding ones. So, the city was expanded two fifth of its size. After the death of Theodosius, subsequent Emperor Marcianus in 451 invited the Kadıköy Council to get together, with this unity, the Archbishop of Constantinopolis were respected in equal highness of the Pope.

An aerial view of Topkapı Palace.
An aerial view of Istanbul.

Therefore, the Church also was divided into two as East and West. Leon l, who took over Marcianus' reign, invited lsaurians to get rid of Aspar the leader of German Community in the Capital and Isaurians having easily dominated the city, shortly took over the government on the name of their commander Zenon and ruled for 15 years. In the meantime, Western Roman Empire was swept away from the stage of history in 476 as a result of German attacks. Anastasios l, who took over after Zenon, while trying to balance the economy, caused conflicts among religious communities as a result of his discriminative attitude towards religion. Trying protect his crown by extensive privileges given to the Orthodox community, Justinianus 1 (527-565), nephew of Justinius, who took over right after him, reorganized the army and went for crusades to enlarge the borders with respect to the former extent, therefore on his victory over the Vandals and Berberis in Africa, Goths in Spain, rearranged the contemporary map of the region as Mediterranean Sea to be a lake for Eastern Roman Empire. However, he received disregard on his performance because of his suppressive regime.

Galata Bridge from Eminönü.
View of the Sultanahmet and St. Sophia.

Orthodoxes, The Blues who were the rep-
resentatives of land-owners and The
Greens who were the representatives of
trademen and craftsmen gathered in
Hippodrome and rebelled against
Justinianus.

During this rebellion dated 532 and
named as Nika Rebellion, St. Sophia previously restored by Theodosius ll as it had
been destroyed before in a rebellion in 404,
was burnt. This rebellion spread throughout the city and a lot of blood was shed.

Following Justinianus, during Justinius ll,

Leander's Tower
The silhouette of Istanbul at sunset.

View of the Bosphorus Bridge at night.
View of the Haydarpaşa at night.

Tiberius 1 and Mavrikios reigns, Constantinopolis gained more importance each day being a milestone on the Silkroad of China-India trade route. The city resisted the attacks from eastern Sasanians and those attacks continued until 591.

In Phokas Period (602-610), religious and political turbulence started again until Herakleios who took over in 610 changed the policy and shared the Anatolian land among the military executions called Thema. Instead of paid soldiers, with the army gathered from Syria, Palestine, Egypt and Armenia, he regained the land once lost. The state which is widely known as

Byzance instead Eastern Roman Empire, had to bear the Arab attacks in 7th century; in 673-677 Arabs kept the city under conquest.

Justinianus ll, who took over in 685, performed a policy based mainly on peasants and therefore, the aristocrats united with the Blues in 695 dethroned Justinianus'll and Leontios became the Emperor. This was followed by Tiberius' counter rebellion and dethroned Justinianus was recrowned in 705. Emperor Justinianus continue to lead the reign until 711 when he was killed in a rebellion. While the Arab attacks were continuing, Theodosios lll became the Emperor. However his reign also didn't last long and in 717 Leo lll was throned. Leo lll supported Iconoclastic attitude and had the busts of previous emperors broken.

The Aqueduct of Valens.

View of Tekfur Palace.

The turbulence was persistent during the reign of his son, Constantinos V. The city endured Arab and Bulgarian attacks and had hard times during this period until the taxes paid to them were increased and trouble was suppressed. From 802 till 811, Emperor Nikephoros l went over Bulgaria several times to get rid of the risk, however, he was killed there. Although Arabs and Russians recaptured the city in 821 during Michael ll period, they were unable to occupy it.

When Basileios, who was a Balcan Slavian, converted to Christianism and making his life as a horsebreaker in Constantinopolis, had the emperor executed and announced himself as the Emperor of Eastern Roman Empire, his Macedonian reign, took over the Byzantine throne in 867-1056. In 963, Commander Nikephoros Phokas ll took over the Empire from Romanos ll. Commander Nikephoros Phokas ll went eastwards and occupied Klikia, Cyprus and Antioch. Then expanded upto Donau via Bulgaria and was killed when he returned to Constantinopolis in 969. After Nikephoros Phokas ll, loannes (Tsimiskes) l took over. While the struggle between aristocracy and peasants were going on, the state was under presssure with attacks from Seljuks on the east, Normans on the west, Petchenegues and Koumans on the north. In a period when Roman and Byzantine churches were gradually alienated towards each other, the public throned Romanos Diogenes in 1068. Diogenes went over Seljuks on the east to get rid of their challenge however in 26th August 1071 was defeated in Manzikert and submitted to Alparslan. When the Emperor returned to Constantinopolis being set free by the Turks, he was killed after his eyes were removed. Taking over in 1081, Emperor Alexios started the reign of Comnenos dynasty. As a result of Turkish threat on the east, Byzance supported crusades on the name of Christianity. In 1096, the first

The walls of Istanbul.

crusaders arrived Constantinopolis having destroyed Hungary and Balcans, the Emperor directed this army to Anatolia. However those first crusaders were tremendously defeated by Seljuks. The same year, the second crusaders started off and captured Antioch in 1098 and Jerusalem in 1099. Independent crusaders and the Byzance had conflicts as the crusaders would torture the common people and destroy wherever they stepped on. That was a reason for rebellion against them within the Empire and Andronikos became the Emperor in 1183 following the rebellion. The outstanding performance of the Emperor was to put pressure on the aristocracy saying "Give up injustice or your life". That motto widely received respect from the public. However the aristocrats united with the outer forces got hold of Cyprus and Sicily; then they went over Constantinopolis. Under such a pressure, the public rebelled against the Emperor and lynched him. When Jerusalem was occupied by Selahattin Eyyubi in 1187, the third crusaders started off. Th e fourth crusaders apt to go over Anatolia, captured Constantinopolis and occupied the city. Therefore the

View of Beyazıt Square.

Byzantines had to fight with the Latins but were defeated and the city was destroyed. Latins declared Baudin the Count of Flander as the first Latin Emperor of Byzance. The new Emperor kept one fourth of the Empire and shared the rest among Venetians and other crusaders. Therefore, three eighth of the land, the Bosphorus and the sea belonged to Venetians. The inhabitants were kept under pressure and they seemed to accept the Latin dominance. The grandsons of Emperor Andronikos 1, established the Pontus Byzantine State in Trabzon in 1204. Contemporarily, an exile government was established in İznik (Nicaea) by Theodoros Laskaris. Kouman Turks and Bulgarians defeated Latins in Edirne (Adrianople) in 1205. Then Constantinopolis had been a colony of the Venetians, until it was occupied by Michael Palaiologos Vlll, the Emperor of Nicaea. That concluded the Latin dominance over Constantinopolis performing a dual policy between Venetians and Genoeses the Empire declared Galata to be a free trade zone and Geneoses were appointed to govern the zone. When

Andronikos ll from the Palaiologos dynasty was throned in 1282, the Empire was suffering a depression in economy and a turbulence in military. Venetians and Genoeses were in a limitless freedom to govern. When Catalans' leader Roger de Flor came to capture Anatolia from Turks but defeated in 1303, he compensated his defeat by plundering Constantinopolis. In the same period, Anatolian Seljuks'state, capital of which was Konya, dispersed under Mongolian invasion in 1308.

Following the dispersion, there were several independent "Beylik"s in Anatolia. One of them was the "Kayı Aşireti" in "Söğüt" under "Osman Bey"s leadership who started the establishment of the Ottoman Empire later in 1299. Ottomans gradually transformed from a small "Beylik" to an expansive Empire and they attacked to conquer Byzance several times. However, in 1453, Byzance was conquered thoroughly by young Ottoman Sultan, Mehmet ll the Conqueror, while Byzance was under the rule of their last Emperor, Constantinos Palaiologos XI.

Several views of Bosphorus.

BYZANTINE WORKS IN ISTANBUL

At the time when the Turks conquered the Byzantium, Constantinople was in the midst of a period of hardship and neglect. As stated by Constantinus and Justinianus, the city was divided into 14 sections. These sections were connected by many roads. The most significant ones were those leading from Beyazıt to Aksaray, from there to Cerrahpaşa, from Altınmermer to Yedikule. Scattered on these roads were numerous squares. The first square which Septimus Severus had built on the hill of Topkapı was adorned by several temples. The Goth Column in the Sarayburnu gate of this square place which Gladius ll Goticus (268-270) had erected in memory of the victory he won against the Goths still erects today.

The second one is the Augustaeum square built by Constantinus. This square which Justinianus requested to be done more sumptuously is marble covered with two-storeyed porticos at sides and a monument of the emperor riding a horse takes place at the center.

The St. Sophia Church is situated at this place. To the west of the St. Sophia Church there were the Patriarch's residence, several inns, to the east the Senate building, to the south two palaces and some Turkish baths. The hippodrome was in the southeastern part of this square. This splendid hippodrome which Septimus Severus had

An aerial view of St. Sophia.

A view of St. Irene.

commenced and Constantinus had completed was a magnificent building for 30.000 people with a sumptuous Emperor's Lodge of 500 m length and 118 m width. The hippodrome had a platform called "Spina" in the center of the racing tracks, The spina was adorned with works of art. The Four Horses Statue which sits at the entry of the Santa Marco Church in Venice today, once originally stood here. To the east of this platform Constantinus VII Prophyregenetos had the 20.68 m high "Örme Sütun" (Plaited Column) built in 994, however, since the bronze reliefs that once adorned it have been removed by the Latins in 1204, only naked stone can be seen today.

Constantinus had the "Burmalı Sütun" (Twisted Column) taken from its original place in the Apollo Temple in Delphi and erected it between Dikilitaş and "Örme Sütun". The column consists of the interwound bodies of snakes with three snake heads on top. The most impressive monument of the hippodrome is the "Dikilitaş" (Obelisk) that Theodosius 1 had brought from Egypt in 290 to be erected here. Displaying the victories of Phorao Tutmosis lll, this 18 m high obelisk has a marble socket with reliefs of Theodosius and Arcadius.

Turks did not give any harm and it was maintained in its original shape until today. Prior to Çemberlitaş, there is the Milion Square which is a small square with the basilica on top of Yerebatan Palace opening to it. The Forum Constantinus in Çemberlitaş, the city's

19

Mosaics of Great Palace,
Byzantine. Istanbul Mosaic Museum.

the column is still maintained in "Kadın Sokağı" (Woman's Street) in Haseki. The reliefs of Emperor Arcadius and Theodosius are being displayed in the Istanbul Archaeological Museum today. The "Kıztaşı" (Maiden's Stone) Column at the Marcianus Square in Fatih is well preserved to this day. The "Mese Street" that started in front of the St. Sophie Church and ended in Edirnekapı with columns on both sides, and behind them covered colonnade section, where shops took place connected all these squares.

The "Great Palace" to the southeast of the St. Sophia Church and Hippodrome that was built during the reign of Constantinus and extended in the Justinianus Period was abandoned in the 13th century and the court moved to Blekarnai Palace. In the Mosaic Museum at the lower part of the

second hill, is surrounded by two-storeyed porticos and in its center is the 57 m high, 9 piece column with the Apollo statue that Constantinus had brought from the Apollo Temple in 328. As Sultan Mustafa ll had it encircled by a hoop to prevent its collapse, this column has become known as Çemberlitaş (Hooped Stone) up to date. On the third hill of the city, which is called Beyazıt today, there was the Forum Tauri that developed in the period af Great Theodosius and there was a silver statue of Emperor Theodosius l on top of a column. Many roads led to this place in the heart of the city.

In Cerrahpaşa was a square named after Emperor Arcadius. As the slave market was held here, Turks called it the "Women's Market". Being one of Istanbul's seven hills, it hosted the column erected by Arcadius to symbolize his victory against the Goths in 402. A part of the pedestal of

View of Pammakaristos Church.

The Pantocrator Monastery which Ioannes Komnenos (1118-1143) had built in Zeyrek suffered a looting during the Latin invasion and only the church division of it could preserved. Following the invasion it was converted into the Zeyrek Mosque. The Chora Monastery in Edirnekapı was built by Emperor Alaxi 1 Komnenos' mother in-law, Maria Doukania between the years 1077-1081, then restored in the period of Annikos II and expanded due to enclosures made between the years 1315-1321 of which the mosaics were done by Theodoros Metokhites. Today, it serves as Kariye Museum.

The St. Nicolas Church in the vicinity of Kariye Monastery was converted into Kefeli Mosque in the Sultan Selim 1 period and

Mosaic of Christ, Pammakaristos Church.

Sultanahmet Mosque, the mosaics of the Great Palace are displayed. The only part of the Blekarnai Palace which was situated between Ayvansaray and Eğrikapı that could preserved until today is the Tekfur (Prince) Palace built by Manuel Komnenos 1 (1143-1180) in the farthest corner in Edirnekapı. When Sultan Mehmet the Conqueror conquered Byzantium, he did not interfere with the religious beliefs of the people and let the churches and monasteries all over the city continue freely with their worship. The Pammakaristos Church built in 1292 was expanded in 1315 when enclosures were built by order of Mikhael Glabas' wife Maria. This church of which the main cupola is adorned with mosaics portraying Jesus and his 12 apostles was converted into Fethiye Mosque during the reign of Sultan Murat lll in 1586. This church in the Çarşamba district is open to visit as museum today.

View of Süleymaniye Mosque.
View of Golden Horn (Haliç).

the church which Leon l had built in Ayvansaray in 458 in the name of St. Pierre and St. Maria was converted into Atik Mustafa Pasha Mosque during the reign of Sultan Beyazıd ll. The church Justinianus had built in 527 dedicated to St. Serge and St. Bacchus in the Cankurtaran district was converted into St. Sophia the Minor Mosque by Sultan Beyazıd ll. One of the most impressive buildings of the Byzantium, without doubt, is the St. Sophia Church. lts construction was started during the reign of Constantinus and was opened to worship on 15th February 360. During a revolt against Emperor Arcadius in 404 this church was burned down and was rebuilt by Theodosius ll in 415. The new church also was destroyed by a fire that accompanied the Nika revolt in 532 and the present church was built in its place during the Justinianus Period in 537. After the conquest, the St. Sophia Church was converted into a mosque and Sultan Beyazıd-ll. and Sultan Murat lll had minarets added. Throughout the course of history it was repaired numerous times and today serves as a museum. The St. Irene Church behind the St. Sophia Church of which the construction dates back to the beginning of the 4th century and completed in the Constantinus period was also destroyed during the Nika revolt in 532, later in the 6th century Justinianus had it rebuilt in its original design.

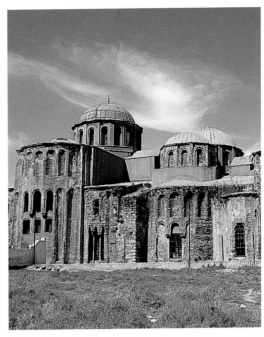

Pantocrator Monastery.
View of Eminönü and Karaköy.

The Fenari İsa (Jesus) Mosque at Vatan Caddesi (street) is the Lips Monastery that was built in the name of Virgin Mary in 907. It was looted during the Latin invasion and turned into a mosque by the order of Beyazıd II.

The Akateleptos Church in Şehzadebaşı that dates back to the 11th century was converted into Kalenderhane Mosque by Sultan Mehmet, the Conqueror and the Hagios Theodorus Church built in Vefa in the 11th century was converted into Vefa Church Mosque by Molla Gürani after the conquest. also the Theodisia Church situated between Unkapanı and Ayakapı was converted into Gül Mosque under Selim II and the Hagios Andreas Church in

Molla Zeyrek Mosque.

Obelisque and Minarets of Sultanahmet mosque.

Cerrahpaşa belonging to the 7th century was converted into Koca Mustafa Pasha Mosque. The İmrahor İlyas Bey Mosque situated between Samatya and Yedikule originally was a monastery, built in 463, but it was converted into a mosque in the Beyazıd II period.

Besides these religious monuments there are impressive cisterns that the Ottomans inherited from the Byzantium and preserved until today. The remains of the Valance Arch, also called Bozdoğan Arch, situated between Edirnekapı and Beyazıt was built by Emperor Valance to solve the tap water problem of Constantinople in 368, consists of a 20 m high wall.

Opposite the St. Sophia Church the Yerebatan Sarnıcı (Underground Cistern) that Byzantine Emperor Justinianus had built in the 6th century, measuring 140x70 m in among the most important works reached to the present day. It was used for some time by the Ottomans and after being restored it was opened to the public as museum. Situated between Sultanahmet and Beyazıt, opposite the Justice Palace takes place the Binbirdirek Cistern which was built by the order of

Philoksenos, a Senate member in Constantinus l period in the 4th century. This cistern measuring 66x56 m was carried by 224 columns consisting of 16 rows each one having 14 columns. Apart from these covered cisterns there were many others like Actius and Aspar that were not covered.

The Kızkulesi (Maiden's Tower) in Salacak, Üsküdar which has become a symbol of lstanbul, was built by the Greek commander Alkibiades in 419 B.C. for the observation of the probable enemies that may come from the Black Sea. The Byzantine Emperor Komnenos converted this tower into a fortress. Kızkulesi, playground of

Views of Galata Tower.

many mythological stories, was rebuilt by the Ottomans and restored as a wooden tower. When this wooden tower burned down, the stone tower that can be seen today was built during the Ahmed lll period and its management was assigned to the Lighthouses Office in 1857.

The Galata Tower, built by the Genoeses as principal tower of the Galata walls in 1348 is 61 m high and consists of 12 floors inclusive a cellar. lts roof has been restored and is being used as a restaurant today.

While many of the Byzantine churches have been restored and preserved as mosques, many churches like Hagia lrene, Fethiye and Kariye and primarily the St. Sophia Church today serve as museum for tourists. Besides these splendid Byzantine buildings, the walls of lstanbul has been restored for many times over the years in order to be maintained for the future. For the first time the walls of Constantinus

Sultanahmet at sunset.
Silhouette of Istanbul at sunset.

encircling five hills were extended during the Theodosius ll period in 412 to cover new districts. These walls started from the shores of the Marmara Sea extending over a distance of 5 km. up to the Golden Horn shore.

Supported by 110 towers, these walls were 15 m high, and strenghtened by a double wall and pits on the land side. The walls of Istanbul have many gates such as Topkapı, Eğrikapı and Edirnekapı. Restoration works that started during the Ottoman Empire period have continued ever since in order to carry these treasures for generations to come.

26

LEANDER'S TOWER

This tower was built during the reign of Ahmed III. It is said to be the site of a Byzantine fortress built during the reign of the empreror Manuel Comnenos, which was itself on the site of a tower built off the coast of Salacak in 410 B.C., by the Athenian Commander Alkibiades. The present tower has been used as a lighthouse since 1857. The tower, also called the maiden's tower, acquired this name through its connection with a legend of the Byzantine era. The emperor Constantine is said to have been told that his daughter would be killed by a snake bite, whereupon, he had her encarcerated in a tower, which was especially built for her offshore. However, a snake hidden in a basket of fruit was accidentally carried to the tower and caused the death of the princess.

Views of Leander's Tower at sunset.

Views of Underground Cistern (Yerebatan Sarayı).

Head of Medusa from the Underground Cistern.

UNDERGROUND CISTERN

Located opposite Hagia Sophia, is the last cistern constructed by Byzantium emperor Justinianus the first in the VIth century.

The cistern having dimensions 70 x 140 m. and with a depth of 8 m. covers 28 x 12 that is 336 columns totally, each of them having a Corinth style capital. Part of it still constains some water.

View of the Sultanahmet Square.

SULTANAHMET SQUARE

The area now overshadowed by Sultanahmet Mosque was, during the Byzantine period, the scene of horse-racing in the hippodrome.

The hippodrome first built by Septimus Severus, and enlarged by Constantinus, was flanked on three sides by tiers of seats for spectators. The Imperial stand was situated on the site of what is now the "German Fountain". Originally it was an arena for wild beasts then a ditch was built around it to protect the spectators from these animals. Later when such games were abandoned a long terrace (called the Spina) was built in the centre, upon which

were set up the Dikilitaş (Obelisk), Burmalı Sütun (Spiral Column), and statues showing a man in combat with a lion, a dying bull, a Hercules by the sculptor Lisippos of Chios, an unruly horse, and an eagle grasping a snake.

The hippodrome, which was 118m wide and 370m long, had high walls. It had a capacity of 100.000 spectators, and had entrances through both of the long walls and also the Antiochus Portal, below the Emperor's Loggia. Forty rows of seats supported by arcades lined the arena. The stairs to the tiers and the circular promenade above them were decorated with statues. The Emperor Wilhelm Fountain (Alman Çeşmesi) now occupies the site of the what was Emperor's Lodge, from which the Emperor and his court would watch the games.

Here he rested, dined, and received visitors. The gallery in front of this lodge was tower-like, and decorated with four bronze statues by Lisippos of Chios.

The silken banners which adorned the Imperial Lodge as protection against the sun were seemingly the augurs of the games, and after preperations were completed, the spectators would gather in the hippodrome at an early hour to watch the combat between the greens and the blues, taking sides in each combat, and fiercely supporting their champions, even to the extent of fighting amongst themselves. It is said that at this stage the emperor would retire to his place along a raised traverse until the uproar had died down. Eventually these games were forbidden, and the hippodrome was used only on days of festival.

It is believed that during the Latin occupation of Istanbul, the statues of the hippodrome were torn down, metal plaques melted down for re-use, and the finest works removed to the west. For example; four bronze horses now decorating the façade of St. Marco in Venice. By the time of the Turkish conquest of Constantinopolis, (now İstanbul) the once grandeous hippodrome was largely abandoned and now in ruins.

German Fountain, 1898.

THE OBELISK

Two obelisks facing one another are still to be seen in Sultanahmet square. One of these, which is inscribed with Egyptian hieroglyphics was brought to İstanbul from Egypt by the Emperor Theodosius, and set up in its present position in the hippodrome. It was given the name the column of Theodosius, and is 18.45m in height, 24.87m including the base. It is constructed of Syenite porphyry, weighing 200 tons, which is supported on a marble plinth measuring 2.75x2.20m.

The plinth is decorated with bas-reliefs showing the life of Theodosius. The northern face shows the Byzantine emperor Arcadius together with his wife, Eudocsia, seated in the Catizma of the hippodrome. The western face shows the Emperor Theodosius, enthroned, together with his wife and his children, Arcadius and Honorius.

Before them are the defeated enemies of the empire. On the eastern face, the Emperor Theodosius is shown watching the games together with his two children,

Theodosius and Arcadius reliefs on the pedestal of Obelisk.

View of Obelisk and Walled Obelisk.

while on the southern face, the Emperor Theodosius is shown with his two sons on one side and on his left Valantinian ll, watching a chariot race.

This column was transported by sea, then, brought to its present site on a specially constructed road, and according to an inscription was set up in 32 days with the help of scaffolding.

The hieroglyphics are to the glory of the Pharoah Tutmosis ll who had the obelisk set up in lower Egypt in 1547 B.C., in the city of Hierapolis.

In brief, the content of these hieroglyphics is as follows: on the eastern side, "Tutmosis lll, of the XVlll Dynasty, master of Upper and Lower Egypt, on the thirtieth anniversary of his reign, as conqueror of the seas and rivers, has set up this obelisk for countless anniversaries to come".

On the southern face, it reads; "With the strength and approval of the god Horus, Tutmosis". "Tutmosis, the all-powerful and all-just son of the Sun, ruler of Upper and Lower Egypt, has penetrated as far as Mesopotamia, at the head of his armies, has shown his might on the Mediterranean, and has fought great battles".

One the western face it is written, "Tutmosis, son of the Sun, who bears the crowns of Upper and Lower Egypt on his brow through the strength, might and wealth of Horos, after paying tribute to the god Amona built this work for his father, the god Amon-ra, that it may spread light like the rays of the sun to mankind".

On the northern face, it reads "Tutmosis paid tribute to the god determined to enlarge the borders of his country as far as Mesopotamia".

View of the Sultanahmet Square.

The walled Obelisk .

THE WALLED OBELISK

At the rear part of Sultanahmet Square is the column set up by Constantine Vll. The obelisk, of coarsely-hove blocks is 32m in height, and formerly was reputedly decorated with bronze plaques depicting the victories of Basil 1, the grandfather of Constantine (867-886) and was crowned with a sphere.

Unfortunately, however, these bronze artefacts were said to have been melted down by the Latins for use in the mint.

SERPENTINE COLUMN

This column, was brought to lstanbul by Constantine the Great from the temple of Apollo at Delphi. lt had been presented to the temple of Apollo by the 31 Greek cities as a token of gratitude for their defeat of the Persians in the battle of Platea, during the Medic wars. A golden vase was set on top of the column, and the column was in the form of three snakes inter wound, and was 8m in height including the three snake-heads which appear towards the top of the column at a height of 6.5m records show us that these snake-heads were in place at the beginning of the 16 th century after which they were broken off. One of the heads is to be found in the Archaeological Museum, lstanbul.

Views of Constantine's Column and Serpentine Column.

CONSTANTINE'S COLUMN

The column of Çemberlitaş, was situated in the old Forum of Constantine the Great. This column, which is 57m in height, was brought from the Apollo temple in Rome and set up here. lt is believed that originally a statue of Apollo greeting the dawn surmounted it, which was replaced by Constantine the Great in 330 with a statue of himself. The column was made of eight porphyry drums which were wreathed with laurel. The statue of Constantine surmounting it was later replaced with a statue of Theodosius, which was dislodged by lightening in 1081. The column was restored by Alexius l Comnenus and an inscription engraved on the capital with a gilded cross in place of the statue. Later, during the reign of Mustafa ll (1695-1704), after a severe fire damaged it, the sultan had a layer of stone added to the base and iron hoops fixed around it, taking its present name from this feature, -the "hooped column"- Çemberlitaş.

THE CHURCH OF ST. IRENE

Aya İrini, as it is now known or the Church of Saint lrene is an important Byzantine church both from the point of view of architectural history, also it is the and second largest church after Ayasofya.

The church lies next to the walls of Topkapı and was used as an ammunition depot until Fethi Ahmet Paşa, Marshal of Tophane had it opened as a museum in 1850. ln 1869 it became the Museum of the Palace (Müze-i Hümayun). ln 1875, the works in this museum were transferred to the Çinili Köşk of the Topkapı Palace.

Exterior and Interior wiews of St. Irene.

The church, which was built by Constantine the Great who consecrated it to the "Divine Peace" was burnt down during the Nika revolt of 532. The Emperor Justinian had the building rebuilt and enlarged. However, it was severely damaged during the earthquake of 732, and during the latter part of the 8th century.

The building is domed basilica, the dome measuring 15m in diameter and 35m in height. From the exterior the dome apears to be rather squat and irregular, whereas in fact it is quite spherical. Many of the 20 windows in the drum were later blocked up. From the exterior, the apse is triple - façaded. lt is semi-domed and has a gilded floor. During the period of lconoclasm figurative mosaics were forbidden, only cruciform motives were allowed.

The building underwent restoration at the apse during that period. The dome was born by piers linking the main nave to the transepts. lt has three tunnel-vaulted naves with galleries over the main piers. The stone work of the wall is typical. Today the building which is connected to The Ministry of Culture is not only an important architectural monument but it is also famous as the first building to be used as museum in Turkey.

THE CHURCH OF ST. SOPHIA

The earliest of Istanbul's church was constructed during the reign of the Emperor Constantinus in basilical form, with a wooden roof. It was then the cathedral church of the city, and entitled Megala Ekklesia. From the Vth century onwards it became known as the church of Divine Wisdom - Hagia Sophia.

The original church was burnt said to have been during an uprising on 20th June, 404, was rebuilt during the reign of Theodosius ll, and re-opened on 10th October, 415. The second church was destroyed by fire during the Nika uprising in 532, and was completely restored with the support of the Empress Theodora, wife of Justinianus after that uprising had been suppressed. The emperor commissioned the architects Anthemios of Tralles and lsidor of Miletus to rebuild it, and according to the account of the

Byzantine historian Prokopius, the emperor ordered a building of great stature and magnificence, using his imperial authority to ensure that nothing was lacking in the building of it. Eight columns of red por-

An aerial view of the St. Sophia

phyry were brought from the Diana Temple at Ephesus. Other marbles were obtained from classical sites and from some of the finest marble quarries of the Byzantine world. A thousand masons and ten thousand apprentices worked on the building, the aim being to finish it as soon as possible. The work began in 532 A.D., was completed in five years, 11 months and 10 days, and the church was consecrated on 27th December, 537 by the Emperor Justinianus.

The grand piers over the underground cisterns on the site were, to some extent, a measure against earthquake damage, but did not prevent this monumental structure from suffering some damage during earthquakes in 533, 557 and 559. We learn that it was restored in 562 by the architect Isidoros, nephew of the earlier architect of the same name, who raised the previously depressed dome by some 6.25m. Further support for the major piers was provided by buttresses.

In the 9th century, during the reigns of the emperors Theophilos and Mikhael III, the bronze doors were installed. In 869 and 889, the church was damaged by earthquake, and was reopened after extensive repair on 13th May, 994. Mosaics were added during the reign of the Emperor Basileios II. During the Latin invasion of

1204, St. Sophia was raided and stripped of its finest ornaments, including the doors, which were mistakenly believed to be gold. The building was greatly damaged during this invasion. Four major buttresses were added to the building in 1317, but it underwent considerable damage later in the earthquake of 1346, to be restored once again in 1354 by the architect G.Prella.

Mehmet the Conqueror had the church restored once again after the conquest of İstanbul, and converted it into a mosque. Among the many restorations and additions to this, the largest church of the Byzantine era, one of the most extensive

Exterior and Interior views of St. Sophia.

Interior views of St. Sophia.

was the addition of buttress walls on the north and south façades in 1317 by Adronikos ll. The four minarets, one on each corner of the building were added at various times during the Ottoman period, the southeastern minaret dating from the reign of Mehmed ll, the northeastern minaret to Bayezid-II and the two minarets on the western façade to the period of Selim ll. The last restoration, carried out during the Ottoman period, the southeastern minaret from the reign of Mehmed II, the northeastern minaret to Bayezit II and the two minarets on the western facade to the period of Selim II. The last restoration, carried out during the Ottoman period coincides with the reign of Abdülmecid. The church was converted into a museum during the recent Republican period, by order of Mustafa Kemal Atatürk, and re-opened on 1st February, 1935.

The building covers an area of 100x70m., and the plan consists of a wide central nave flanked by two smaller naves, an apsis, an inner and outer narthex and a central dome up to 55.6m in height. Owing to restorations carried out at various periods, this dome is no longer entirely circular but has, gradually become elliptical. The forty lobes of the dome, separated by brick ribs, are pierced by oculi. In the centre of the dome are inscribed verses from

The Comnenos mosaic, 12th century.

Mosaic of the Empress Zoe, 11th century.

the Koranic text - the Sure-i Nur, executed by the Ottoman calligrapher Kazasker Mustafa Izzet Efendi.

The interior of the church is of extreme importance to art historians, being finely decorated with a number of important mosaics and artefacts from various periods. According to accounts of the late classical period, it was decorated with fine mosaics of gold, silver, glass, stone, marble, limestone, granite and terra cotta tesserae.

Some of the more important mosaics are as follows: Entering the main portal to the inner narthex, one sees, over the portal, the figure of the Madonna holding the Christ child, flanked by constantine the Great on her right, presenting a model of the city of Constantinople to her, and on her left, the Emperor Justinianus presenting a model of the church. This dates from the last quarter of the 10th century and the reign of the Emperor Basil ll. The cross-vaulted portico to the inner narthex is decorated with gold mosaics of the Justinian period. These are the original non-figurative mosaics of St. Sophia, which, being non- figurative, released from damage during the lconoclastic period.

The Emperor's Gate, on the south-western façade of the church is surmounted by a mosaic showing Christ enthroned on a semicircular encrusted throne, holding a book. The medallion to the right of this contains a bust portrait of the Madonna, and to the left, a bust of Gabriel. The figure prostrating himself before Christ is thought to be the Emperor Leo, and the mosaic is thought to date to the 10th century A.D.

The semi-dome of the apse contains a mosaic of the Madonna enthroned, holding the Christ child, dating to the 9th century. It is thought to be the earliest figurative mosaic on the Posticonoclastic period in the church. To the right of the drum stands the white-robed figure of Gabriel, and to the left, nowadays considerably damaged figure of the archangel Michael. Portraits of the saints once decorated the semi-circular arched niches below the northern tympanum, only three of these have survived.

On the western wall, contained in the niches, are portraits of the partiarches of the eastern church, the İstanbul patriarches, Saint lgnatius and loannes Kryostomos in the first and central niche, and the figure of Saint lgnatius Theophoros, patriarch of Antakya (Antioch) in the fifth niche.

These figures are robed in mantles bearing cruciform motifs on the collar and skirt, and hold the bible in their hands. The names of the figures are written beside them in Greek. These mosaics date from the end of the 9th century to the beginning of the 10th century. The four pendentives

of the dome are decorated with the figures of cherubim or seraphim. Those on the eastern side of the church are original, while the western figures were restored in fresco in 1847 by Fossati.

Access to the galleries of the church is obtained via a stone-paved ramp. The gallery decorated with green columns directly opposite the apsis was used by the empress and her retinue during ceremonies.

Entering the southern gallery from here one passes through a pseudo-wooden marble door, now named the gate of heaven and hell. The right-hand side, decorated with floral motifs representing heaven; the left-hand side, undecorated, representing hell.

Passing through this door one enters the chamber set aside for the meetings of the consuls, decorated with the Deesis mosaic,

Deesis mosaic, 12th century.

one of the most famous mosaics in the world. It portrays Christ flanked by the Virgin and John the Baptist. This extremely expressive mosaic dates to the 12th century. In the gallery to the southeast of the Church is to be found the Comnenos mosaic, in which the enthroned Madonna and child enthroned are flanked on the left by the Emperor Ioannes Comnenos II holding a pouch of money and on the right by the Empress Irene, a Hungarian princess.

The figure of the Madonna is surmounted by a monogram describing her as the mother of God, while the names of the other figures are inscribed next to them in Greek. In one corner one can also sees the mosaic portraying the sons of the Emperor Ioannes (John) Comnenos II, and his co-ruler Alexius Comnenos. The latter is shown in a frontal pose, in elaborate gown and crown, and holds a sceptre in his raised right hand. On the northern wall of the emperor's hall, in the southern gallery

The Virgin Mary and Justinian Mosaic.

is to be found the Zoe mosaic. The empress stands to the right of the enthroned Christ with her third husband, the Emperor Constantine Monomachos IX on his left. The mosaic dates to the 11th century A.D.

The mosaic of the Emperor Alexander can be seen on the southwestern end of the central hall on the northern gallery. Alexander, the third son of Basil I, who ruled for 13 months in 912, is shown standing, facing forward, elaborately dressed in ceremonial robes and crown. In his left hand he holds an orb, and in his right hand a pouch. His name and titles are inscribed in two medallions on either side of his head. Dating to the Xth century AD, this mosaic is in reasonably good condition. After seeing these extremely important mosaics, we will have completed our tour of the St. Sophia Church, except for the grounds where one may see the monumental fountain built by the Ottoman Sultan Mahmut I.

The Deesis Mosaic.

An aerial view of Chora Monastery.

CHORA MONASTERY (KARIYE MUSEUM)

The building known today as the Kariye Museum was the Monastery of Chora which dates from the Byzantine age. It was built outside the city walls of Istanbul in the district of Chora, and called "Monits Choros" - or simply "Chora". The monastery was built by Theodorus in 534, during the reign of Justinianus but later suffered considerable earthquake damage. In the 12th century it was rebuilt by order of Maria Dukaina, the mother-in law of Emperor Alexi Comnenos and was dedicated to Christ. By the 14th century the building, which had greatly deteriorated, was completely restored and adorned with mosaics by Logothere Theodore Methochite the Great, he spent his entire fortune for this purpose. After Mehmed the Conqueror captured Istanbul, the building remained as a church. But later Hadim Ali Paşa, the Grand Vizier of Bayezit II, converted it into a mosque, and added a minaret in 1511. A religious school (medrese) was also built next to the mosque, which, from that time on known as "Kariye". During the Republican period the monastery was turned into a museum and its mosaics were uncovered by the American Institute of Byzantine Research. In addition, the area of Kariye was recently restored very successfully, by the Turkish Touring and Automobile Club and is now open to visitors. The building, with dimensions 20m x 28m x 50m, has an inner and outher narthex on the western side, a cemetery chapel on the south and a gallery on the north. The floor and the inner narthex are covered with marble, creating a very striking effect. The building has a large central dome and five cupolas surrounding it. Let us now take a look at the mosaics, which have preserved their beauty since the 14th century: Over the inner wall of the outer narthex portal is a mosaic depicting the Madonna and Child. Next to this, a large mosaic, above the portal to the inner narthex features Christ the "Pantocrator". On either side of his head are inscribed the letters which make up his emblem. Following the museum plan, mosaic No. 1 is on the northern wall to the left of the portal and shows the Holy Family going to Jerusalem to attend the feast of the Passover. Mosaic No. 2 features the Holy Family returning to Nazareth from Egypt. St. Joseph is bearing Jesus on his shoulders. To the left of the mosaic St. Joseph is depicted being told to

The Virgin Mary and her ancestors.

return to Nazareth in his dream. In mosaic No. 3, an angel is depicted informing St. Joseph that Christ is about to be born, and we observe Mary in conversation with Elizabeth and the Holy Family returning to Bethlehem. The 4th mosaic, on the vault, shows figures of the saints. No. 5 features the Census being carried out under Cyrenius supervision, and mosaic No. 6 shows the birth of Christ. Angels and children attend the event. In the lower left hand part of the mosaic women are washing Jesus Christ while Joseph is standing to the right. Above the door, the 7th mosaic features the miracle of Christ transforming water into wine and multiplying loaves of bread. The frescoes No. 8 on the wall above the portal are of a later date. In the second part of the vault is depicted the Priestess Irene Paulina Paleolilina and

Mosaic of Governor Cyrenius.
Mosaic of Theodoros Metochites.

Jesus and Virgin mosaics.

members of the imperial dynasty. The centre of the vault features mother Mary and Christ accompanied by the Saints. Vault C depicts the wise men before King Herod.

In section No. 9, the Blessed Elizabeth is fleeing from the soldiers with St. John in her arms. No. 10 features King Herod ordering the massacre of all new-born babies. No. 11 depicts the Massacre. Let us now go to the western part of the vault and see mosaic No. 12 on the plan, which features Jesus Christ and the Samaritan woman.

Representations of various saints are to be seen on the western part of the vault. On the eastern wall of the outer narthex, marked "D" in the plan, is a large scale mosaic of the Madonna believed to have been which was destroyed during the

49

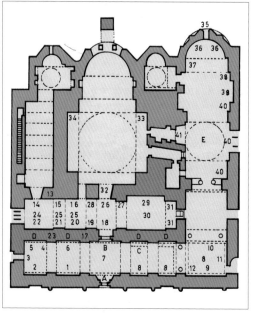

Mary and child Jesus in the dome.
Plan of Chora Monastery.

Byzantine period. We can now proceed to the inner narthex, that northern part bears mosaics depicting the life of the Virgin. The one shown as No. 13 features St. Joachim in the Desert, Lamenting his childless state. No. 14 depicts the angel's Annunciation 7, the birth of Mary. No. 15 shows the couple embracing with delight. No. 16 features Mary's birth while No. 17 shows the first steps of Mary, as a child.

In Panel No. 18 on the opposite wall, Mary is buying wool for the cover of the Tabernacle, No. 19 shows the chief priest praying in front of the scepters deposited in the temple before selecting Mary's future husband. No. 20 features Joseph's sceptre from which leaves are sprouting, an indication that he is the prospective husband. The mosaic No. 21 shows Joseph taking Mary to his house No. 22 depicts the farewell scene between Joseph and Mary. No. 23 shows the Annunciation within a medallion. On the northern dome, No. 24, are depicted Mary and her ancestors, while on the vaults (No. 25) are: the tutoring of Mary by the High Priest, the procession of virgins, Mary's presentation to the temple, and the Saints. Mosaic No. 26, above the portal to the church properly features the presentation of a model of the Church to Christ by Theodore Metochites, the Patron of the church. No 27 to the right of the door shows St. Peter and No. 28 to the left, St. Paul. Panel No. 29 at the left depicts

The frescoes of the Angle and Anastasis.

Christ and the Virgin. Below right is Maria Paleologina, daughter of Emperor Michael VII and member of a religious order. On the same level towards the left is Isaac Comnenus, third son of the Emperor Alexi Comnenus.

The southern dome, No. 30, features the line of Christ, and the mosaics at the end wall (No. 31) show Christ's miracles and the saints. Let us now enter the main church. Mosaic No. 32 above the inner portal depicts the death of the Virgin.

Mosaic of St. George.

Opposite, No. 33 on the right hand side, is the Madonna bearing the child Jesus. On the left, No. 35 features Christ bearing an open book, the page bears the inscription "let all those who suffer come to me". The first fresco (No. 35) on the semi-dome of the side gallery is the Anastasis fresco. Below this are six saints, and on the soffit of the arch Gabriel. The vaults (No. 37) above the altar feature the "last judgement", below which Hell is depicted on the left and Heaven on the right.

The frescoes shown as No. 38 feature Christ and the Virgin, and above them are representations of the miracles of Christ, Following these (No. 39) a group of four figures, including the Nun Eugenie and the Priest Macarius. Fresco No. 40 shows the Saints, the inscription of Tormikes, saints again, a figure bearing a candlestick, and the Wise-Men in worship.

Opposite, No. 41 features the saints, the raising of Israel, and on the dome the house of Mary. On the pendentives are depicted poets and the authors of the Bible. Other churches presently open to the public as museums are: the old Church of St. C. Studius which is now called "Imrahor", and the Church of St. Mary Pammakaristos which is presently known as the "Fethiye Museum". The latter was been converted into a mosque in 1587 during the reign of Murad III. Its narthex which bears the mosaics is now open as a museum.

The Jesus mosaic on its ceiling has remained intact to this date. The Church of St. Irene in the first court of Topkapı Palace was built by Justinianus adjacent to Haghia Sophia. It is the second largest church in Istanbul of the period. At present it is being used as a museum.

A general view of the dome depicting the genalogy of Christ.

THE ISTANBUL ARCHAEOLOGICAL MUSEUM

The lstanbul Archaeological Museum is one of the most important museums of its kind in the world. Founded as a museum during the Ottoman period, then the imperial museum, the collection includes a number of findings from various parts of the Ottoman empire, including Mesopotamia, and in particular such monuments as the Alexander's Tomb, the tomb of the weeping maidens and the Lycian Tomb found at Sayda in Syria in 1891.

Originally the museum collection was exhibited in the Çinili Pavilion, an annex of the Topkapı Museum now in use as the

Views of the İstanbul Archaeological Museum.

Relief of a lion.
View of Çinili Pavilion.

museum of faience and ceramics and dating to the period of Mehmed ll. But as the collection grew, the present building was erected between 1892-1908, to which a later annex has been added in recent years. The late 19th century museum building was inspired in style by the tomb of the weeping maidens.

The museum collection include up to 60 thousand archaeological findings of various kinds, nearly 500 thousand coins and medallions and nearly 75 thousand cunciform inscription tablets. It is among the greatest collections in the world. The collection can be seen in three separate sections. In the Museum of the Ancient Near

55

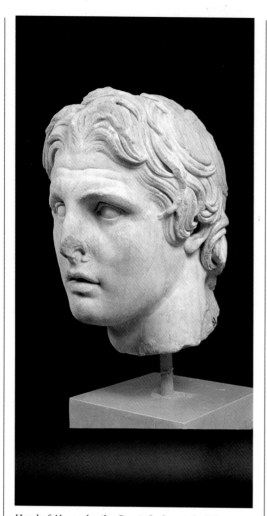

Head of Alexander the Great, 2nd century B.C.

its from the walls of the palace of king Tiglat Pileser at Nemrut.

In other parts of the museum are displayed seals and hieroglyphic tablets from Mesopotamia and works of the Urartu and Phrygian periods. The Hittite period, (dating from 2000-1200 B.C.) in Anatolia, is well represented, and the works on display includes those of the Hittite imperial period, and of the later Hittite city states, (dating after 1200 B.C.) Among the most notable works of the period to be seen are vessels of various kinds, bronze axes and the hieroglyphic tablet inscribed with the text of the famous "Kadesh Treaty".

Late Hittite works of note include the Zincirli reliefs, the Maraş findings and the famous Babylonian reliefs, decorated with bull, dragon and lion figures in brickwork,

Caryatid, Early Roman period.

East, which stands opposite the main building, in the classical section housed in the main building and in the Çinili Pavilion. On entering the Museum of the Ancient Near East, the first hall houses Egyptian artefacts, tombs and mummies among them. In halls III and IV, one may see work from Mesopotamia, including findings from Halef, Nineva the periods of Old Sumerian, classical and New Sumerian and the Gudea statues. In the section containing works of the Assyrian period, one can see the statues of Puzur Ishtar, governor of Mari. His son and Salmanasar III, and reliefs of winged spir-

56

Statue of Marsyas, 3rd century BC.

First of all, let us visit the halls on the right hand side where statues of ancient times take place. Works of the first gallery are of archaic period. In the second gallery the works of Anatolia under sovereignity of Persians between 546-333 B.C. and in the third gallery, the Attic grave stelae and reliefs of 6-5 century B.C. take place. In the following gallery, works of Hellenistic Period (330-30 B.C.) adorn the hall.

In this hall, beautiful heads and a statue of Alexander who initiated the period take place. One of the heads was found in Pergamon and draws attention with its hairs in form of a lion's mane. Based on the portrait of Alexander the Great made by Lysippos in IVth century B.C., this type of hair is peculiar to Alexander. This particular portrait a work which was made in

Statue of Nymphe, 1 st century B.C.

which was removed from the walls of the ceremonial way and the lshtar gate at Babylon. Classical section of the lstanbul Archaeological Museum is taking place among noted museums of the world, upon completion of the new additional building in 1992 has rearranged and opened to visitors.

Entrance with triangular frontal supported by four pillars is reached by white marble stairs. These stairs lead to hall way where the statue of God Bes of Roman Period takes place. In the galleries on both sides of this hallway connected to each other with halls the master pieces of the world are being exhibited.

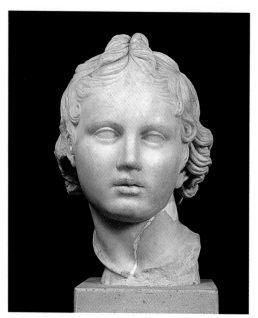

Bust of a child, 1st century.

Pergamon sculpture shop in 2nd century B.C. Again, in this hall Marsyas' statue, the Roman period copy of the work of 3rd century B.C. can be seen. As it is known God Apollo punished Marsyas by flaying his skin, for entering in a musical contest with him.

This is the statue which illustrates Marsyas hung on a tree for punishment. Also the statue of Zeus and a huge divine statue which most possibly belongs to Attalos ll, the King of Pergamon of 2nd century B.C. found at the Temple of Hera of Pergamon are most remarkable ones.

In the fifth gallery the statues found in Magnesia of Meander (Menderes River) and Tralles (Aydın) are being exhibited. Right across the hall from the door the Statue of famous Ephebos (young athlete) takes place.

This statue which was found in Tralles and belongs to the Early Roman Empire Period depicts a child athlete of about twelve years old while resting, tired of sportive activities he had gone through. The statue

is illustrated with a pelerine thrown over the short clothing.

At the right hand side of the door the statue of Apollo, Goddess heads, statue of a half naked Nymphe can be witnessed. On the left hand side, the statue which belongs to a woman named Balbia, of 1st century B.C., statue of Athena, woman's statue and various statues of women and men take place.

On the left side of the passage way (Carian) leading to the other hall, a statue of a woman found at Tralles and used as a pillar attracts the attentions. As the examples encountered at the monument of Nereids in Xanthos near Fethiye and at the monument of Limyra near Finike, these

Statue of young Athlete, late 1st century B.C.

Statue of Oceanus, Roman period.

statues have been used in place of pillars in various locations.

From here, it is proceded to a hall where examples of Roman sculpture art are displayed. Right in the center poetess Sapho's head made in Roman Period is located, on the right, statues of Aphrodite and Cybele, on the wall the relief made in the name of Euripides author of Tragedia, reliefs of Mousa playing guitar take place. To the left of the hall are the examples depiciting the Roman art of portrait. Here, the busts of Augustus, Tiberius and Claudius of Roman emperors and the statues of Neron and Hadrianus take place. In addition, the statue and the bust of Marcus Aurelianus, the bust of Empress Faustina and other men and women busts adorn the hall.

On the right hand side of Aphrodisias' Hall named after Prof. Kenan Erim who made excavations for a long time at Aphrodisias and died in 1990, Statues of Roman judges and the statue of a woman are being exhibited. Aphrodisias is near Karacasu county in the province of Aydın

in Western Anatolia. The Sculptors here when Attolos lll, King of Pergamon left his territory to Rome in 133 B.C. migrated to Aphrodisias the capital of Caria region and here created marvellous works out of the marbles obtained from the rich marble quarries. These statues of Aphrodisias sculptor school were exported to Greece and Rome. On the walls of this hall, take place the reliefs illustrating the war between the Gods and Giants. Today, the works obtained in excavations in Aphrodisias are being displayed in the local museum.

Works found in Ephesos can be seen in the center of this hall. On the floor, statue of Oceanus, the God of Rivers, next to it

Head of Arcadius, 4th century A.D.

Sarcophagus of the Weeping Maidens, 350 B.C.
Statue of the Valentianus II, 4th century.

the statue of Polemaeanus, the proconsul (Governor) of Asia found in Celsus Library of Ephesos take place. On the left hand side of the hall, the works found in Miletos and on the opposite wall the statues found in the Faustina Bath are exhibited. These are the musical muse playing flute, statue of Melpomene and the God Apollo playing guitar. In the next hall, works of Roman Empire Period are seen. Next to the works found in Anatolia, also, the works found within the boundaries of Ottoman territory of those days are exhibited. Heads of Poseidon, Artemis, Statues of Zeus and Tykhe, the Goddess of good luck are among those works adorning this hall. In

the gallery on the left hand side of the entrance leading to the museum of sarcophagi beautiful one from another are being exhibited. Right across from them, is sarcophagus of King Tabnit of Sidon made out of black stone. From the inscription thereon, it is decided that the sarcophagus belongs to General Peneftah lived in time of 26th family in Egypt and used for King Tabnit of Sayda for the second time. On both sides of this sarcophagus, Egyptian and Greek type sarcophagi take place, magnificent Lycian sarcophagus behind them dates back to 5th century B.C. and was found in Necropolis of King of Sidon.

This sarcophagus called Lycian sarcopha-

Statue of Artemis, Roman period.
Lycian Sarcophagus, 5th century B.C.

Hunting scene on a face at the Alexander sarcophagus.

gus due to its resemblance to the sarcophagi of Lycian region was found at Sidon by Osman Hamdi in 1877 and brought here. On one side of it a lion hunt and two carriage each drawn by four horses, and on the other side a boar hunt are illustrated. On narrow sides the fight of Kentoros and Lapith and a scene of fight between the Kentoros over a deer can be seen. Behind this sarcophagus which is a work of a Lycian sculptor takes place a satrap's sarcophagus again brought from Sidon. On this work which belongs to the later part of 5th century B.C., the life of a governor general of Persia called Satrap is illustrated. After an intervening section we arrive a hall where Alexander's sarcophagus is. This sarcophagus with its splendor comes in sight in the center after going by three other.

This sarcophagus made out of white marble and bears fine reliefs in fact does not belong to Alexander, but it is called by this name due to his war and hunt scenes thereon. This sarcophagus with an 2.12m height, 3.18m length and 1.67 m width shows; Alexander's battle with Greeks as the subject for the illustrations on narrow surfaces thereon.

One at the left end is the illustration of Alexander. On the other there are the scenes of lion and deer hunts. The wounded lion in the center of hunting scene is

Details of Alexander Sarcophagus.

illustrated in the act of biling. Also the cavalier to the left of the lion is Alexander himself on his head, he wears a hand having the royal symbol. The sarcophagus which belongs to 4th century B.C. is shaped like a temple and displays a delicate stone labor which arouses administration with its painted and high reliefs.

Behind this sarcophagus takes place the sarcophagus of Weeping Women. On this sarcophagus made for a Sidonian in 350 B.C. there are eighteen sad women. They are separately illustrated to get rid of

Gold pendant head-gears, Troy II, 3000 B.C.

monotony. On the top cover two identical funeral processions are illustrated. In this department, there are the halls of the museum which shall be reorganized. On the upper floor of the newly opened part of the museum, the Anatolian Civilizations. Through Ages' Exhibition is on display. On the left side of the hall the works of Troy can be seen.

City of Troy burned down and rebuilt nine times is at a distance of 30 km from Çanakkale. This city also has been inhabited from 3500 to 300 B.C. without interruption. Therefore it is possible to follow the cultures of periods parading one after another.

First excavation in Troy which occupies an important place in history for reasons of being the first site of excavation in Anatolia, constituting subject for Epic Poems of Homeros, and giving a firm chronology, was made by Schliemann in 1870. Story of excavations and colorful personality of Schliemann made Troy so much more important. After him Dörpfeld continued the excavations. Later, starting in 1932 American Belegen carried out this job, works being exhibited are the ones found during the excavations made by Schliemann and Dörpfeld.

İznik blue and white Mosque Lamp, 16th century. Çinili Pavilion.

OTTOMAN PERİOD

In spite of the strong resistance for all those years, following a conquer of 54 days, Sultan Mehmet, the Conqueror invaded Byzance on 29th May 1453. As the Emperor Constantinos XI died in panic, the Turks got hold of the city within two hours. The panic throughout the city calmed down in three days and the Sultan ordered the submission of the ones who escaped and were hidden. He guaranteed the public would keep living as the way they used to in terms of their religious and traditional practices. He also asked someone to be elected for the vacant Bishop

İznik Lamp and tile, 16th century.

position. When Georgios Skholarios was elected as the bishop, Sultan muted him for dinner and rehonored the Bishop with the Crown and sceptre of the church. Havariler Church was appointed as the official residence for the Bishop and his community.

On first Friday in the city, Sultan Mehmet, the Conqueror went to St. Sophia Church for his Moslem religious practices. Then he decided to restore the city and to keep it as a focus point of the contemporary world. Firstly the walls surrounding the city were repaired.

Monasteries and the churches were converted to Mosques and "mescit"s (small mosques). The elites of the city were allowed to build mosques, "medrese"s (schools), "imaret"s (houses to deliver free food), "darüşşifa"s (hospitals), "hamam"s (baths) and "bedesten"s (bazaars) wherever they would like to build them. Therefore, these gave a new impetus to the city. Sultan Mehmed, the Conqueror had his first palace built in Beyazıt, where University of Istanbul stands today, how-

66

ever later on he had Topkapı Palace and the walls surrounding it built in 1462-1478 and left his first palace to move in the greater new one.

Sultan Mehmed also had "Fatih Külliyesi" Fatih Complex built on the fourth hill of the city in 1463-1470 and "Eyüp Monument-tomb and Mosque" in memory of Ebu Eyyub El Ensari who died in Arab Conquer. To improve the trade within the city, "İç Bedesten" (interior market) was built and that is the core of today's "Kapalıçarşı" (Covered Bazaar). By the end of 15th century the quantity of temples, baths, schools and the buildings of that kind was about 300. The destroyed city was restored. The public surrounded by

İznik Tile and Tankard, 16th century.

the walls, no matter which ethnic group they belonged to, led a peaceful and free life in terms of their traditions and religious practices. An internal castle called "Yedikule" (Seventowers) was built to keep the treasury.

Sultan Mehmed, the Conqueror died in Gebze in 1481 on his way to expand the country borders by conquering new land. His son Beyazıd ll was throned after him. Fatih rests in the monument-tomb nearby the Mosque built during his life. In 1488 during the reign of Beyazıd ll there had been frequent earthquakes. 109 mosques and 107 houses were destroyed and the losses were great. Fatih Mosque was also destroyed by an earthquake and it was restored later on. During this period of restoration, Sultan Beyazıd ll had Architect Yakup Shah Bin Sultan Shah built "Beyazıd Külliyesi" on Forum Tauri square of ancient Byzance in 1501-1506.

Following the death of Beyazıd ll, Yavuz Sultan Selim was throned and went over Çaldıran and Egypt, therefore Islamic "Caliphate" was handed to Ottoman

Empire from Egypt. Sultan Süleyman the Magnificent, who took over from Yavuz Sultan Selim (1520-1526), had Sultan Selim Mosque built on a "Haliç front" hill in memory of his father in 1522-1526 and the great Yavuz Sultan Selim rests there. The famous architect Mimar Sinan, contemporary of Sultan Süleyman the Magnificent first built Şehzade Mosque in memory of the Sultan's son Prince Mehmed, in 1543-1548, then in 1550-1557 Süleymaniye Mosque on a hill above Golden Horn.

Mimar Sinan designed the silhouette of the city with the buildings known as Mihrimah Mosques, one of which stands at the end of Beyazıd-Edirnekapı Arch and built in

View of Şehzade Tomb (1648).
İnterior view of Selim II Mousoleum. (1577).

An aerial view of Sultahahmet Mosque.
Interior view of Rüstem Pascha Mosque (1561).

1562-1565 and the other in Üsküdar built in 1548. He also built Rüstem Pasha Mosque at Eminönü by the Golden Horn in 1560 and this mosque has the quality of a Tile Museum.

Süleyman the Magnificent entitled Mimar Sinan to find a solution for water shortage in the city and he built the Moğlova and Güzelce additional to the Halkalı Aqueduct to transfer water from Belgrad Forests to the city. Sinan had a long life during which he could have the opportunity to serve several Sultans. In 1551, for wife of Süleyman the Magnificent, Hürrem Sultan, he built "Haseki Külliyesi"; in 1571, for Sokullu Mehmet Pasha, he built "Sokullu Külliyesi" at Kadırga. Moreover, in Beşiktaş, Sinan

View of Mihrimah Sultan Mosque, Edirnekapı, (1565).

Paşa Mosque and Külliye (1553-1555) and Cihangir Mosque (1559) were also built by him.

When Sultan Süleyman the Magnificent died in Zigetvar in 1566 while he was away on command of his army for the 13th time, his corpse body was brought to İstanbul and buried in a monument-tomb, built by Mimar Sinan besides Süleymaniye Mosque, to rest in peace. Selim ll who took over after him, had Mimar Sinan built Selimiye Mosque in Edirne.

When Selim ll died, hisbody was buried at St. Sophia in a monument-tomb built by Mimar Sinan in 1577. Sultan Murad lll was throned in 1574 and there was a spectacular celebration of the circumcision rit-ual of Crown prince Mehmed at At Meydanı (Horse Place).

The Sultan watched these celebrations from the İbrahim Pasha Palace which serves as lslamic Works Museum today. During the long-lasting festivities, the vendors' procession paraded and clowns entertained the people. These events have been reflected quite frequently in the Ottoman miniature art.

When the Sultan died in 1595 he was buried in the monument-tomb built by Architect Davut Ağa in the garden of the St. Sophia and his son Mehmed lll took over. After a succession of sultans who did not go to war since the death of Süleyman the Magnificent, he led the army into battle, conquered Eğri Castle, won the Haçova war and returned to lstanbul. When Sultan Mehmed lll died in 1603, he was buried in a monument-tomb built by Dalgıç Ahmet Ağa at the St. Sophia Church in 1608 and his son Ahmed 1 (1603-1617) became the sultan.

In tradition with the monuments created by Architect Sinan, Sultan Ahmed had

Interior view of Fatih Mosque.

70

Exterior and Interior views of Eyüp Mosque (1798).

Architect Sedefkar Mehmet Ağa build Sultanahmet Mosque with 6 minarets opposite St. Sophia between the years 1609-1617. The mosque was fitted with a cupola of 36.6 m diameter and 43 m height and the interior was adorned with Nicaea glazed tiles in the 17th century. Together with a "medrese" and "türbe" it was treated as külliye. In this türbe are buried Ahmed 1, Osman ll, Kösem Sultan, Mustafa IV and their children.

Following Sultan Ahmed 1, Mustafa 1 was throned. He was found incompetent after a short while and replaced with the 14 year old Osman ll named Genç (Young) Osman because of his young age but he was killed in a revolt of "Janissaries" and "cavalry sol-

diers" and Mustafa 1 was throned again in 1622. But since he was mentally deranged, he was toppled soon after, and Murad IV took over. Between the years 1623-1640, Murad IV reigned who successfully smothered upheavals and disciplined the army by undertaking expeditions to Iran, Baghdad and Revan.

In memory to them, the Revan and Baghdad Kiosks were built in Topkapı Palace. Meanwhile, one fifth of Istanbul was destroyed in fire that broke out in Cibali. The building that Safiye Sultan ordered architect Davut Ağa to Build Eminönü was started in 1657, upon his death was continued by Mehmed Çavuş and finally in 1663 Turhan Hatice Sultan had it completed by Architect Mustafa Ağa.

This mosque and "külliye" as well as the Mısır Çarşısı (Bazaar) that was conceived to finance it where the best of their kind built in classic style in İstanbul. In the tomb of this "külliye" are buried Turhan Hatice Sultan, Mustafa ll, crown princes and the distinguished individuals of that time. In the 17th century, following Murad IV Sultan İbrahim was throned in 1640,

but since he was incompetent he was dethroned in 1648 and Sultan Mehmet IV took over. At this time sultan mothers like Kösem Sultan and Turhan Sultan had gained great influence over the throne, and during the reign of successive sultans the Ottoman Empire's old glory slowly diminished.

While revolts continued to break out, Köprülü Mehmed Pasha was appointed Grand Vizier in 1657 and succeeded in reinstating state's authority. Following the reigns of Süleyman ll, Ahmed lll and Mustafa ll, in the 18th century Sultan Ahmed lll came to power between the years 1703-1730 and during his time, referred to

View of Nusretiye Mosque, (1826).
Interior view of Nuruosmaniye Mosque (1755).

View of New Mosque. (1664)
The fountain of Ahmet III. (1728)

as "Tulip Era", peace and entertainment prevailed. This sultan had Mehmet Emin Ağa build the Ahmed lll Fountain in front of Topkapı Palace in 1728. Civilisation activities continued with the İskele Fountain built in Üsküdar in 1728 and Ahmed lll library built in the Topkapı Palace. Also, the first printing house was founded by İbrahim Müteferrika in lstanbul. However, this era ended with a revolt led by Patrona Halil in 1730 and Sultan Ahmet lll was dethroned.

Mahmud l, who was throned after Ahmed lll in 1730 had Architect Mehmet Ağa built a fountain in Tophane in 1732 and the foundation of Nuruosmaniye Mosque was laid in 1748, but upon his death it was completed

Küçüksu Pavilion (1853).

by Osman lll. Following Osman lll, Mustafa lll took over and later Abdülhamid 1. Following his death, Sultan Selim lll, who known for his love of art, was throned in 1789.

This Sultan who was at the same time a composer, decreed the "Janissary Fraternity" as useless and set out to design a new and disciplined army. Thus an army called Nizam-ı Cedid (New-order) was founded in 1792. Those opposed to his reforms revolted under the leadership of a strongman named Kabakcı Mustafa and dethroned and killed Selim lll in 1807, installing Mustafa lV in his place.

Alemdar Mustafa Pasha led a campaign to

lstanbul to take revenge of Selim lll, but since Selim lll had already been killed, he dethroned Mustafa lV and helped Sultan Mahmud ll take over. After arranging for a big funeral for Selim lll he had his murderers killed. His tomb is in Laleli, where he is buried side by side with Mustafa lll. A pestilence, brought to lstanbul from lzmir by a ship in January 1812 caused the death of thousands of people.

Thereafter lstanbul was devastated by a smallpox epidemic in 1825. The reformist Sultan Mahmud ll had Nusretiye Mosque built in Baroque style in Tophane and the construction of Selimiye Garrison was completed in 1829. Sultan Mahmud ll ordered initially, the army, members and then the people to wear a "fes", sort of a hat, to adapt European clothing to the Ottoman life-style. During his reign the first daily news paper, Takvim-i Vakai, was published and the first Military School was founded.

When Mahmud ll died in 1839 he was succeeded by his 16 year-old son Abdülmecit l, who had a tomb built for his father in

Malta Kiosk in Yıldız Park.

Yellow Pavilion in Emirgan Park.

His tomb takes place within the Sultan Selim Külliye. When Sultan Abdülmecit died at a young age, Sultan Abdülaziz took over who is the first sultan to make a journey to a foreign country upon the invitation of the French Emperor. He had Beylerbeyi Palace built at the Anatolian side of the city, Çırağan Palace at the European side, the Yıldız Palace and the Valide Mosque in Rococo style. When Sultan Abdülaziz died, Sultan Murat V took over, reigned for a short period and was succeeded by Sultan Abdülhamit ll, who had quite a long reign.

This sultan abandoned Dolmabahçe Palace to settle in Yıldız Palace and in addition to Yıldız, Valide, Çit, Malta, Şale, Büyük Mabeyn kiosks and others such as Bahçıvanbaşı, Talimhane, Av Kiosks, Küçük Mabeyn and Harem were built, thereby expanding the palatial area considerably.

When Abdülhamid was dethroned on the advent of the 20th century, Sultan Mehmed Reşad V took over and after having the neglected Dolmabahçe Palace

Ihlamur Pavilion (1855).

Divanyolu where he was buried. During his reign, the Foreign Minister Mustafa Reşid Pasha announced the "Tanzimat Fermanı" (Reforms Decree) in 1839 intending to adopt the Turkish people to western standards. He left Topkapı Palace and had Dolmabahçe Palace built in place of the wooden Beşiktaş Palace between the years 1843-1856 where he moved thereafter. Architectural progress was significant and saw the completion of lhlamur Pavilion in Beşiktaş in 1855, Göksu Pavilion in Küçüksu, Ortaköy Mosque in 1853, Teşvikiye Mosque in 1855 and the mosque in Baroque style built for his mother Bezmialem Valide Sultan next to Dolmabahçe Palace.

repaired he moved there. He was buried in the tomb built by Architect Kemalettin in Eyüp after his death in 1918. The Ottoman Dynasty ended as Mehmet Vahdettin Vl, who was throned after Mehmet Reşad V, left the country on board of an English vessel in 1922. The Ottoman Empire, being defeated in World War l dissolved and Anatolia was divided up between the invading nations. Mustafa Kemal led and won the lndependence War against the invading nations. ln 1923, the Parliament (Great People's Parliament of Turkey) determined Ankara as the capital of the young Turkish Republic.

Detail of Çırağan Palace Gate.
View of Çırağan Palace (1863).
Ortaköy Mosque (1853).

MUSEUM OF TURKISH AND ISLAMIC ARTS

This museum situated in the historical palace of lbrahim Paşa, opposite the Sultanahmet Mosque, and opened in May 1983 after 15 years of restoration.

This unique collection was previously on display in the imaretsoup kitchen of Süleymaniye Mosque, but has now moved to its new location where vast, new display opportunities are afforded to the museum. The lbrahim Paşa Palace is situated by the Hippodrome, the site of various ceremonies and games during the Byzantine

Jeweled Gold Turban ornament, 17th century.
Detail of Jeweled ivory belt.

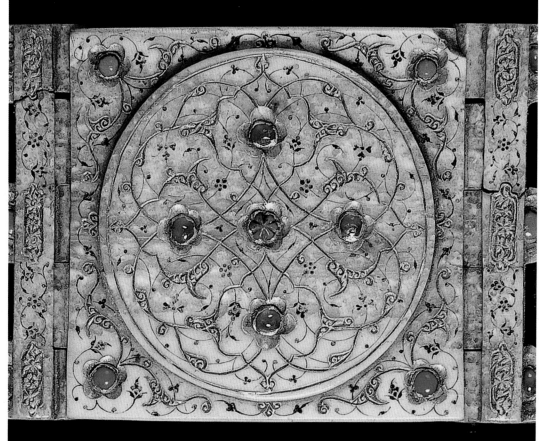

Gold necklace, 19th century.
Enameled Gold Turban ornament, 17th century.

period, and also during the Ottoman period, when the Hippodrome was re-named the Horse Parade Ground - At Meydanı - The Palace was most probably the site of the tribunes of the arena.

Although we do not know exactly when this stone building was originally constructed, a document in the archives of Topkapı Palace refers to its restoration in 1520, which indicates that the palace must pre-date 1520. In 1521, it was presented to İbrahim Ağa, then Paşa, later vizier, by Sultan Süleyman the Magnificent. In 1524, the palace witnessed the 15 days and nights of celebration in honour of the marriage of its new owner, and in 1530, the three-week long cirumcision celebration of the crown prince. After the death of Ibrahim Paşa, the palace remained as the seat of viziers, and was inhabited by a number of prominent citizens in succession.

Miniatures illustrating the circumcision celebrations of crown prince Mehmed, son of Murat III in 1581 are the best source we have for the structure of the palace at the time. These illustrate both the audience to the celebrations and the imperial gallery, the grand divanhane, the deep eaves and terrace grills of the palace façade. The palace also played an important role in the celebrations held for the completion of Sultanahmet Mosque.

Two miniatures from "Zübdet-üt Tevarih of Seyyit Lokman" (1583).

Wooden window shutters of the İbrahim Bey imaret.

Koran Case, 17th century.

The building has survived by the help of several reconstructions, and with the final restorations begun in 1967, it became an ideal setting for the museum.

On entering the palace, one finds an exhibition hall, a gallery of shops and a conference hall on the ground floor. Passing through the turnstile, one mounts a flight of steps to the courtyard, which is surrounded by buildings showing various aspects of traditional Turkish nomadic and settled communities, including handicrafts and woven artefacts of considerable interest, and scenes from the henna night, circumcision, wedding and the Turkish

Carpet, animal patterned, 15th century.

are the pottery vessels and glass goblets, the figurative, unglazed ware, wooden window shutters, metalware and mirrors of the Seljuk period.

The Ottoman period is represented by some very fine artefacts in the collection, dating from the 15th to the 19th century, including manuscripts, silverware, bronze, wooden, faience and pottery, and mother-of-pearl inlay artefacts, the most notable of which are bowls, plates, lanterns, orbs, bowls and ewers, incensers, rose-water sprinklers, candelabra and lecterns.

The rugs on display are among the finest in the museum collection, and these are shown in the divanhane of the museum, where the outsize 16 Uşak rugs and the earliest known Seljuk rugs from the Alaeddin Mosque in Konya are displayed side by side with western Anatolian rugs and large carpets of the 16-17 th centuries.

Ladik prayer rug, 18th century.
Bergama rug of the Holbein type,

baths. A flight of steps to the right of the courtyard lead up to the second floor of the museum, where lslamic artefacts are displayed in chronological order, accompanied by panels giving the background to the collection. The earliest works on display here are 9th century fragments from Samarra, near Baghdad, including wood, stone and frescoes.

From here one enters a larger saloon where works of the Turkish Eyyubid, Mameluke and Timurid periods dating from the 13-15th century, are displayed including Eyyubid pottery from Raqqa, vessels, figurines and lamps, a glass lantern and ceramic ware dating from the Mameluke period, and the 14-15 th century, Also including brass lantern of some importance and pottery, glass lanterns, bowls and goblets, metalwork and Koran manuscripts of the Timurid period. Some of the most important artefacts on display

TOPKAPI PALACE

The palace of Topkapı, which is mentioned in several different contexts in this work, is a group of structures in which are incorporated works from each successive period of the Ottoman age.

It is well known that Mehmed the Conqueror constructed the first Turkish palace in Istanbul at Bayezit, on the site of the present University of Istanbul, but this palace very soon became inadequate for the needs of the sultan and the Ottoman administration, whereupon the order was given to construct a new palace on the promontary overlooking both the Marmara and the Bosphorus, known now as the Seraglio Point. Construction of this palace was begun on the site of an ancient olive grove sometime during the lifetime of Mehmed ll. The final palace covered an area of 700 m², and was enclosed within fortified walls of 1400 m in length.

The walls were pierced by a number of gates, namely the Otluk Gate, the Demir Gate and the Imperial Gate - Bab-ı Hümayun, and a number of minor angled gates between them. After the reign of Mehmed ll, the palace grew steadily to from a city-like complex of buildings and annexes, including a shore palace then known as the Topkapı Shore Palace, as it

View of Topkapı Palace from above.

Entrance gate of Topkapı palace.

was situated near the cannon gate - Topkapı - of the ancient walls of Istanbul. When this palace was burnt down in 1863, it lent its name to the great complex we now know as Topkapı Palace, which had, until then, been known simply as the "New Palace".

The main portal, the Bab-ı Hümayun was situated next to the mosque of Ayasofya (Haghia Sophia), and this led into a series of four courts surrounded by various structures. The first court was the ceremonial court, and contains the earliest structure in the palace, the Çinili Pavilion, which dates to 1473. The second court was entered via the Bab'us-Selam, or the

Middle Gate, and contained the imperial council chamber. This was referred to as the Court of Justice, and the council building, or dome, is situated on the left handside of the court.

This building is a three domed structure containing the council chamber, the chambers of the Grand Vizier and the Imperial Registrar's chamber. Behind it rises the tower of justice, which has undergone repeated restorations, the latest fairly recently. To one side of this building are the barracks of the crested halberdiers, and to the other is the Imperial Treasury. Behind and below them are the royal stables, news and livery rooms. These build-

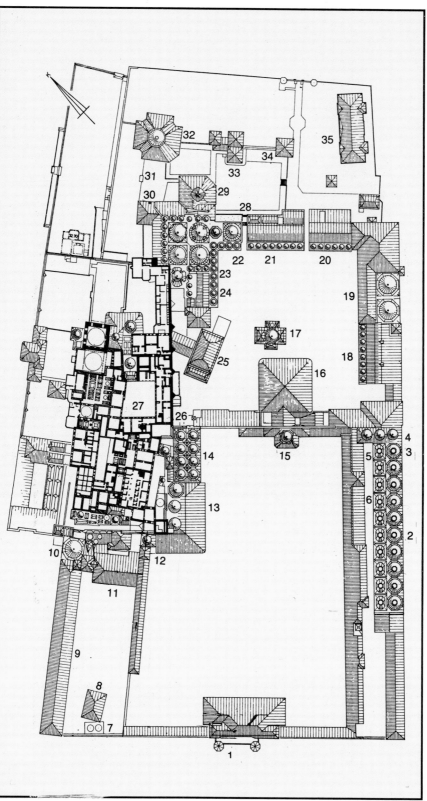

Plan of Topkapı Palace.

1 - Main gate (Babü's selam)
2 - Chinese and Japanese porcelain section (kitchen)
3 - Palace kitchenware section (helvahane)
4 - The Istanbul glassware and porcelain section
5 - The Sami Özgiritli section
6 - Silverwork and the european porcelain section
7 - The Meyyit gate
8 - The Beşir Ağa Mosque
9 - The royal stables
10 - The Raht treasure
11 - Barracks
12 - Entrance to the Harem
13 - The Dome
14 - The Arms and Armour section
15 - Gate of the white eunuchs (Babü's saade)
16 - Audience chamber
17 - Library of Ahmed III
18 - Textiles and kaftans section
19 - The Treasury section
20 - Director of Museum
21 - Royal portrait gallery
22 - The Clocks section
23 - Apartment of the holymantle and sacred relics
24 - Calligraphy and manuscripts section
25 - The Library (Ağalar Mosque)
26 - Gate of Kuşhane, Harem
27 - The Harem
28 - Entrance of the fourth court
29 - Revan Pavilion
30 - The Circumcision room
31 - The İftariye Kiosk
32 - Bagdat pavilion
33 - The Pavilion of Mustafa Paşa
34 - Hekimbaşı tower
35 - The Mecidiye Kiosk

The Sweetmeats Room.

Gold matara and steel helmet, 16th century.   *Gold ceremonial throne, 1585.*

88

The throne of Nadir Shah, 18th century.

Rock crystal matara and flask, 16th century.   89

ings display features attributable to the period of Mehmed ll. The eight -cupolaed lmperial Treasury, with a roof resting on three large piers, is particularly notable amongst them. On the other side of the court are to be seen the kitchens which were constructed after a fire in 1574, and given their present state during the time of Süleyman the Magnificent. From this court one passes through to the third court via the Bab'üs Sa'ade or the Gate of the White Eunuches.

Just opposite to this gate stands the throne room, which dates to 1596, but was restored and redecorated in 1856. To the

The Spoon-maker's Diamond (86 carats).
The Topkapı dagger (1741).

90

Gold cradle.
Ruby pendant.

right of this isolated structure can be seen the four chambered Privy Treasury, also known as the Mehmed the Conqueror Pavilion, which is flanked by the barracks of the Treasury and Cellar Guards, and in one corner of the court are the privy chambers where the sacred relics of the prophet are now on display.

The structures in this court were modified in 1719 with the addition of a third barracks next to the treasury, and the replacement of a fountain kiosk to the left of the throne room together with the library of Ahmet lll.

After the sacred relics were brought to lstanbul by Selim the Grim in 1517, and

The Sacred Relics Chamber.

installed in the privy apartments, an extension to the palace was made in the fourth court. Here, in 1636, Murat IV added the Revan Pavilion, and in 1639 the Baghdad Pavilion, an octagonal structure dominating the seraglio point, and in 1640, Sultan Ibrahim had a circumcision room erected nearby in which faiences dating from the 15,16 and 17th centuries were used for decoration. Beside this is the Iftariye Kiosk.

From this terrace, two steps lead downn into the tulip garden, in which are to be found structures dating to the period of Mehmed II, the Hekimbaşı Chamber of Baş Lala tower, and the pavilion of Mustafa Paşa, also known as the Sofa Kiosk. Three other structures in the same court are the Sofa Mosque, which dates from the reign of Mahmut II, the Mecidiye Pavilion and the Esvap Chamber.

One of the most interesting and important secitions of the palace complex is the harem. Considerable research has been carried out on the origins of this extraordinary group of buildings, and constant restorations have thrown some light on certain aspects of the structure. Among the more important structures in this section of the palace are the Pavilion of Murat III, dated 1578 and attributed to architect Sinan, which is decorated with faience revetments. Flanking this is the Reading Room of Ahmet I, which contains a fountain a niche dated 1608.

The mother-of-Pearl and tortoise-shell inlayed closets and shutters are especially fine. This room gives access to the Fruit Room of Ahmet III, dated 1705, which is an interesting structure decorated with painted lacquer representations of fruit and floral motifs, typical of the period.

On the other side of the Murat III pavilion are the Crown Princes' apartments, also known as Çifte Kasırlar, a two-roomed sec

Interior of the Paired Pavilion, 16th century.

Mihrişah Sultan's apartment.

tion revetted with faience bearing features typical of the 17th century decorative style-fashion. The imperial hall was the ceremonial hall of the harem, which was built after the pavilion of Murat lll, although we do not know exactly when. The faience inscription frieze running along the wall bears the date 1666, and the name of Mehmed IV, but the hall was largely renovated during the 18th century and also during the reign of Osman lll. The ornamentation bears the overwhelming influence of the baroque and rococo styles of that period.

One other part of the harem dating from the reign of Mehmed IV is the apartment of the dowager sultan. Over the portal leading to these apartments we read the date 1667. The faiences in the dowager sultan's bedroom and prayer room are particularly fine.

The room underwent several minor alterations and additions in 17th century, during the period of Osman lll, and later under Abdulhamit l and Selim lll. Some of the

finest examples of Turkish baroque and rococo are to be seen in the chambers beyond the dowager sultan's apartments, in the chamber of Mihrişah Sultan, built in 1790 for his mother by Selim lll, and the flanking music room of Selim lll Also in the bedroom of Abdulhamit l and the pavilion of Osman lll.

Among the other important structures in the harem are the Masjid of the Black Eunuches which contains a faience panel portraying the Kaba, dating to the 18 th century.

The Crown Princes' school, the guard room of the Black Eunuches, is also decorated with faience of the same period, as the Barracks of the Black Eunuches and the hall-with-a-hearth.

View of the Imperial Hall (Hünkâr sofası), 16th century.

DOLMABAHÇE PALACE

When Abdülmecit 1 succeeded to the Ottoman throne, the westernization of the Ottoman empire had already become an important trend which was also felt in the architecture of the time. It was this movement which led the sultan to have the older palace of Beşiktaş demolished and replaced by a new structure more in the western genre. Dolmabahçe was built between 1843 and 1856, and its grand opening was announced in the Ceride-i Havadis newspaper of 11th June, 1856, when, it is said, Abdulmecit took up residence there amidst much pomp and circumstance. The palace contains a selamlık

General view of the Dolmabahçe Palace.
The Treasury Gate, Dolmabahçe Palace.

General view of the Dolmabahçe Palace.
The Clock Tower.

or male quarters, a grand hall, a harem and apartments for the crown princes. The latter is now used as the Museum of Modern Art and Sculpture. In this structure, for the first time in Ottoman history, the selamlık and harem were arranged under the same roof. Among the other important structures in what was still, effectively, a palace complex were the privy treasury, the furnishing rooms, the Paşa apartment, and the apartments of the Eunuches, the Gentlemen - in - waiting, the White Eunuches and the Harem porters, and apart from these were the glass pavilion, and two other pavilions, the Kuşluk Kiosk and the Hareket Kiosk. Besides these, the palace also contained a

Stair Hall, Dolmabahçe Palace.
The Crimson Room.

theatre, a royal stable, a boathouse, store rooms, a chemists and a sweetmeat bakers all outside the high walls of the main grounds. The main gates were the Treasury Gate, situated beside the clock tower and the State Gate. Other important gates were the Valide Gate, the Veliahd Gate, the Koltuk Gate, the Baltacılar Gate, the Mefruşat Gate and the Matbah Gate. The palace itself was a three storey building with two main storeys rising over a half-sunken floor, and contained 285 rooms, four grand saloons, six galleries and six baths. Apart from the service stairs, there were more than five main staircases in the state and harem apartments. The ambassadorial hall, the privy saloon, the Grand assembly hall, the pink

and blue saloon are among the most notable rooms in the palace. The ambassadorial hall was preceded by an envoy's antiroom of some magnificence, and led into the sultan's private ambassadorial audience chamber, which was finely decorated with Vienna porcelains, tiled mantelpieces, silver candelabra and the solid gilded cornice surrounding the room. Fine Hereke rugs add to the effect of the room. The harem ceremonial hall was used as a prayer hall during Ramazan, the holy month of fast, and after the accession of Sultan Reşat, it was also used for banquets. This saloon leads into the marble room and a library. A corridor leading away from the saloon takes one to the music room and to the sultan's bath, which is

The Blue Saloon, Dolmabahçe Palace.

Stair Hall, Dolmabahçe Palace.

finely decorated chamber revetted with Egyptian marble. The harem is entered via a corridor leading from the apartments of the dowager sultan, the sultan's wives and members of the harem. One of the most important rooms in the harem is the pink saloon, which was used by Atatürk as a living room and bedroom, and a small side room which he used as a study. The apartment of the dowager sultan is a 95 m long wing set a right-angles to the harem proper. This three-storey apartmet complex let into the larger saloons via various corridors.

The decorations in this section of the palace are sparse compared to the building, and the original furnishings have largely been removed. The harem and state

One of the Table Clocks in Dolmabahçe Palace Zülvecheyn Saloon.

The Ceremonial Hall in Dolmabahçe Palace.
Silver Vase (Indian Style).

apartments are linked by the Grand Assembly Hall in the centre of the palace, which was used for grand occasions such as coronations and holiday celebrations.

A gallery running across the saloon (room) below the roof was allocated to musicians and foreign envoys. The room is covered by a dome, supported on four grand arches, which in turn are born by four large piers. In the transition to the dome are pendentive stalactites.

Dolmabahçe, like the other Ottoman palaces of the period such as Beylerbeyi Palace and the royal lodge at Küçüksu, reflects the Ottoman Europeanised taste of that era.

Façade of Selamlık section in Beylerbeyi Palace.   *Interior View of Beylerbeyi Palace.*

BEYLERBEYİ PALACE

One of the most important Istanbul palaces is the Palace of Beylerbeyi. It is situated at the foot of the Bosphorus Bridge on the Asian shore and was built between 1861 - 1864 by Sultan Abdulaziz in place of a wooden palace which was previously on the site.

The sultan, who was a keen sportsman and a known artist, is believed to have prepared sketches for the decoration of the palace, which were later used in the decoration of the ceilings. The palace is a three storey structure, and is set in terraced grounds planted with trees brought from all corners of the globe. On the uppermost terrace of the grounds is to be found a marble pool, surrounded by three pavilions, the Sarı Pavilion, The Marble Pavilion and the Ahır Pavilion, each of which is important in its own right.

The harem and selamlık quarters of the palace are situated on the shore of the Bosphorus. The palace is decorated in the style typical of 19th century Europe, and the original furnishings are preserved there, giving the palace the distinction of being a fully furnished museum. The building, in the French baroque style, is constructed of stone and marble. The harem and selamlık sections are in two separate buildings. The lowest storey is subterranean, and above it are two other storeys containing six main rooms and 23 side rooms.

Entrance is via a curved marble staircase into the Harem hall, the largest chamber on the lower floor is known as the pool room, as it contains a large pool in the centre.

Rooms on the lower floor are reached via a door on the shore façade. In one corner of the shore façade is the Captain Pasha room, and in the other two corners are reception rooms. Rooms allocated to the harem as dining halls on this floor were

also used by Abdülhamit II as his privy apartments on his return from Salonika. The most interesting chambers on the upper storey are the inlay room and the magnificent blue room, decorated with blue stucco columns, painted ceiling, inscriptions, chandeliers and vases.

On the garden façade of this chamber are the apartments used by the Empress Eugene during her stay in Beylerbeyi, and on the shore façade is to be seen the mahogeny revetted reception room of Abdulaziz.

From here one may enter the inlay room, which gives onto the panelled, mukarnas niched ambassadorial reception room and the conference room of the palace.

THE MOSQUE OF SÜLEYMANIYE

Süleyman the Magnificent ordered a mosque appropriate to his title to be built by the Architect Sinan, whereupon the present mosque was begun on one of the hills dominating the Golden Horn.

To ensure the absolute stability of the foundations, upon the bed-rock of the site, three years of preperations were made, and three more years passed in the construction of these foundations. Following

Interior and exterior view of Süleymaniye Mosque.

Interior views of Süleymaniye Mosque.

these fastidious preperations, the actual construction of the mosque begun. The mosque, and its attendant structures, madrasa, arms-houses, infirmaries, caravanserais, a medical school, baths, schools of tradition (dar ül Hadis) a hospital (dar üs Şifa), cells and shops were begun in 1550 by the Architect Sinan and completed in 1557.

The architect called it a work of his training period. The truly magnificent mosque now dominates the sky-line of the city from the Galata Bridge. On its completion, it was opened to worship when the sultan and his entire court attended a vast consecration ceremony. The large outer court is entered by 11 portals. The inner court, rec-

Interior view of Süleymaniye Mosque.

tangular in form, is reached through three portals, one central, the others flanking this. The central portal is dressed with fine stonework, and surmounted by an inscription containing the Islamic proclamation of faith. Flanking the portal on both sides are three rows of cells and 12 windows.

The courtyard is paved in marble, and framed by a revak covered with 28 cupolas. In the centre is a rectangular fountain with an ornamented central piece. Two of the four minarets of the mosque which both have two "Şerefe"s (balconies) are situated in the two corners of the northern façade. The other two are to be found on the rear façade of the mosque; these

are taller than the first pair and dressed with three balconies. The total of ten balconies was to indicate that Süleyman being the tenth Ottoman sultan. The mosque itself is almost square in plan, measuring 63x68 m. The height of the dome is 53 m. Entrance is through the central portal of the main façade, and the two side portals, which lead, respectively, to the lmperial gallery and to the public nave.

The central dome rests on four arches springing from four great piers; while a semidome is placed over the mihrab and the entrance portal. On either side of the main dome are five cupolas, supported on pillars set between the main piers, and resting on the arches from these piers. Thus an outstanding area was left free for congregational prayer. On the street to the left of this mosque are situated the primary school and madrasas of the complex, which are now the Library of Süleymaniye; The Medical School on the corner of the street is today used as a Dispensary, while on the opposite side of hospital is today a Military Printing Office.

The magnificence of the mosque, clearly reflected in its architecture, also prevails on the interior, in the fine portal gates, carved marble mihrab and mimber, and even in the carpets, chandeliers and bronze candlesticks. The mosque is illumi-nated by 138 windows which bestow a superb light upon the interior. The mihrab is decorated with blue and white Kütahya tiles and the mosque has an acoustics quality which altests to the mastery of its architect. The materials used in the building of the mosque were brought to the site from the Istanbul area, and even from the farthest part of the empire.

Two of the piers originated from the city of Istanbul, one from Alexandria in Egypt and one from the ruins of Baalbeek. The tomb of the sultan, also the work of Sinan, is an appropriate edifice to the magnificence of all. The tomb, built by Sinan for the sultan on his death at the age of 71, in

Süleymaniye Mosque at Night.

1566, is octagonal, each face decorated with inscriptions and five windows, two below and three attached to the clerestory. The dome of the tomb is ornamented with a marble crested consol.

The tomb is surrounded by a covered gallery resting on 29 columns. The portal door is of ebony inlayed with ivory and decorated with relief work, the walls on either side of the portal with turquoise, dark blue, white, red and harmonious yellow tile panels. Within the tomb, four of the eight columns resting on marble bases are of

Interior view of Tomb of Süleyman.
Detail of İznik Tile in the Tomb of Süleyman.

white marble, four are pink marble. The capitals are decorated with gilded inscriptions. The dome of the tomb is supported on these columns, and this is decorated with designs typical of the period, in which burgundy is the dominating tone.

There are seven catafalques (decorated platforms on which the coffin of a famous person lies) in the tomb of Suleyman, whose own catafalque is the high structure in the centre of the mausoleum.

Flanking this türbe is a second mausoleum, which belongs to the wife of the sultan, Hürrem Sultan, the famous lady who addressed the sultan in her fervour with the words "l would sacrifice myself for one hair from your whiskers."

This is octagonal and preseeded by a rivak. The entrance portal is decorated with faience on either side.

General view of Sultanahmet Mosque.

THE MOSQUE OF SULTANAHMET

Ahmed l, who ascended the throne at the age of fourteen was an extremely religious-minded sultan, who displayed his religious fervour in his decision to construct a mosque to compete with Ayasofya.

For the site, a suitable place was long sought before the decision was taken. At last the mosque decided to build on the site of the palace of Ayşe Sultan. The owner of the palace was compensated and the site prepared by the architect Mehmed Ağa, who began the construction in 1609.

General views of Sultanahmet Mosque.

Interior views of Sultanahmet Mosque.

This architect poet and inlayer completed this great work in 1617. An imperial lodge, school, service kiosk and single and double storied shops were included in the complex, which spread over the area around the mosque.

The mosque itself is surrounded on three sides by a broad courtyard, and is entered on each side by a total of eight portals. The inner court is reached through three gates, and is paved in marble, and surrounded by revaks supported on columns of pink granite and marble, and two of porphyry, and surmounted by 30 cupolas. A fine fountain for ablution takes up the centre of the courtyard, surrounded by six

Interior view of the Sultanahmet Mosque.
İznik tile in Sultanahmet Mosque.

marble columns. The mosque is unique with its six minarets in lstanbul. Four of these have three balconies, two have two balconies each, a total of 16 in all. According to the memoires of Mehmed Ağa, the "Risale-i Mimariye" -the number of balconies was originally to be 14 in honour of the number of Ottoman sultans, but in the 16th century, the number was increased by two, according to lncicyan, to include the sons of Yıldırım Bayezid, Emir Süleyman and Musa Çelebi, who had meanwhile been counted among the sultans. This mosque intended to match and compete with Ayasofya, but in reality surpass it in proportion and the balance of internal spaces. lt covers an area of 64x72 m in all. The central dome rests on four

110

pointed arches with corner pendentives, which are in turn set upon four large round and fluted piers, 1.60 m in diameter. Four semidomes, one to each side of the central dome, and small cupolas in the corners complete the roof-system of the mosque. The sultan's gallery in the left corner is flanked by the penitentiary cell of Ahmed l.

Sultanahmet Mosque is given a bright and open effect through carefully calculated illumination balanced with faience decorating in the interior, as if heralding a new type of architecture. The most original feature of the mosque is the 260 windows through which it is so well lit. Later these coloured windows were repaired and consequently light entering the interior increased. However this is said to have

The tile panel.
Interior view of Sultanahmet Mosque.

The Sultanahmet Tomb.

of his son Osman II. The building is basically rectangular with a domed portico and a square extension at the rear. The entrance rivak is supported on 6 columns, with a cross vault in the centre flanked by a cupola on either side. The ebony doors of the tomb are worked with inscriptions from the Koran.

The plaster windows have been replaced by glass, making the interior very light. The narrow panels between these windows on the interior are covered with 17 th century tiling. These are dark green, dark red, blue and white. The most striking feature of this tiled decoration is a band of inscription in reserve white over a dark blue back ground around the interior.

The dome and walls are plastered. Above the marble mihrab-like niches on the façade facing the entrance are to be found inscriptions relating to the construction of the tomb of Osman II.

This mausoleum contains 36 tombs of various sizes; the central one of which belongs to Ahmet I. In front of the mausoleum a marble-faced clock tower was built during the 19 th century. Behind this is a library.

removed the mystic atmosphere of the interior. According to Celal Esat Arseven, the architect Mehmet Ağa has attempted to create an extremely well lit sofa, (divan area). The walls and piers are covered with faience for a third of their height to the level of the upper consols. A total of 21043 tiles have been used in the interior.

The mosque received its synonym as the Blue Mosque from the blueish haze given to the interior by these tiles.The faience consists of floral and rumi motifs of various colours on white ground. These are very fine examples of the art of tiling. The bronze and wooden decorations and artefacts of the mosque are also very fine. Calligraphy is the work of Ametli Kasım Gubari and the fine mother-of-pearl window shutters are the work of Sedefkar Mehmet Ağa.

Ahmet l died in 1617 and was buried near the mosque. The tomb, which was begun after this date, was completed in the time

İznik tile in Sultanahmet Mosque.

THE COVERED BAZAAR

The foundations of one of the most out-standing covered markets of lstanbul, the Grand Bazaar, which stretch from Beyazıt to Nuruosmaniye, were layed out immediately after the conquest of lstanbul.

The Conqueror first laid the foundations of the old bedesten (market), and these were followed by those of the Sandal bedesten. The bazaar grew from shops and hans, lining the streets, which had the space between covered over for more convenient shopping.

The resulting arcades were covered with roofs and arches, and were illuminated by clerestorey windows. Each street became the centre of one particular trade, such as the street of the slipper - makers, furniture

Different views of Covered Bazaar.

- makers and quilt - makers. The bazaar comprised 4400 shops. 40 hans on over 50 streets, 2200 rooms to the hans, together with business premises, mosques and 19 fountains and hamams, making up what was efectively a city within itself.

The covered bazaar itself consisted of the Bedesten at the centre, which was entered by four main gates, the Gates of the Sahaflar (Goldsmiths), Takkeciler (Cap - Makers). Zenneciler (Fripperies Woman's Garments) and Kuyumcular (Jewellers).

The main streets were named the streets of the Tent - Makers (Çadırcılar), Quilt - Makers (Yorgancılar), Fez - Makers (Fesciler), Fur Hat - Makers (Kalpakcılar), Pouch - Makers (Keseciler), Cap - Makers (Takkeciler), and Nuruosmaniye. These streets were attached to a maze of roads and alleys. The most important of the streets which numbered up to fifty were the streets of the Clog - Makers (Kavaflar), Printed - Clothier (Basmacılar), Sandal Bedesten and Aga Sokak.

Several views of the Covered Bazaar.

The Bazaar underwent a great threat during the fire of 1546 and was later seriously damaged and restored after the fires of 1660, 1695, 1701 and 1750. During the eartquakes of 1766, 1791, 1826 and1894 it was badly damaged, and the Hans of the Market were completely destroyed and closed down. The street of the Kalpakcı between Beyazıt and Nuruosmaniye was closed off by gates at each end over which the Tughra (Coat of arms) of Abdülhamid ll was mounted.

The Covered Bazaar underwent fires during 1943 and 1954 which destroyed much that was authentic. However it still retains

its attraction as the center for Turkish jewellery, carpets embrodery and such like handicrafts.

The market, which began to grow over the foundations of the old Bedesten and later the Sandal Bedesten gradually grew to its present state. The first nucleus of the market, the old bedesten was surrounded by walls 1.5 m thick, covered by 15 cupolas and itself covered an area 45 by 29.5 m, a total of 1336 sq metres.

The four gates of this market opened onto the streets of Keseciler, Takkeciler, Sarraflar and Kuyumcular.

Two views of the Covered Bazaar.

A CRUISE IN BOSPHORUS AMONG HISTORICAL BUILDINGS

The Bosphorus, which connects Marmara Sea and Black Sea, is one of the most exquisite places in the world, with a width of maximum 3.200 m and minimum 550 m, maximum depth of 118 m and its length is 31,5 km. lt was naturally formed at the beginning of the lVth Geological Era as the sea water occupied the deep valley.

During the ages of Byzantine and Ottoman Empire small settlements cropped up at both shores of Bosphorus and it was very much esteemed by the sultans and pashas where they built their kiosks and "yalı"s

(water-side residences) as of the 18th century. Wearing effect of time caused the wooden buildings demolish and they were replaced with new ones.

In place of the wooden Beşiktaş Palaces there appeared the Dolmabahçe Palace and also Beylerbeyi Palace was rebuilt while stone buildings like Göksu were built and gave the Bosphorus its final outlook. With its architecture matching its natural delights the Bosphorus reached and incomparable beauty. The buildings embroidering the shores of free-flowing

View of the Fatih Sultan Mehmed Bridge form Kanlıca.

waters, being embraced by a green background as a whole offer a view of unceasing delight. Such a wonderful cruise will provide unforgettable memories. For this to attend a trip with a tourist ferry taking off from the Eminönü Jetty will suffice. If you have the opportunity to take part in one of the private boat cruises or yachts, the trip will be even more delightful.

Our tourist ferry will start leaving Topkapı Palace, St. Sophia and Süleymaniye Mosque behind. The Karaköy Jetty will be crossed arriving in front of Tophane. Here we see the Nusretiye Mosque, built by Sultan Mahmut ll in Ampiric style in 1825. The lead-covered mosque behind this mosque is a work of Mimar Sinan, who dedicated it to Kılıç Ali Pasha.

Passing Fındıklı and the very lively Kabataş Jetty, the Dolmabahçe Palace appears with its mosque and Clock Tower. The mosque was dedicated to Sultan Abdülmecit's mother, Bezm-i alem Valide Sultan and was built by Mimar Karabet Balyan in 1853. The Clock Tower between the mosque and the palace is 27 m high, and was built by Mimar Serkis Balyan in 1890 during Sultan Abdülmecit's reign. The palace built by Karabet Balyan by the order of Sultan Abdülmecit between the years 1843-1856 is 284 m long, and it is an ornament to the Bosphorus. The palace has three storeys consisting of the men's part, entertainment hall and the harem. The separate premises next to the palace used to be the crown prince's residence and today serves as the Paintings and Statues museum.

Our tourist boat will steer to the Barbaros Hayrettin Pasha Jetty named after the famous Turkish sailor. A bit further there is the Naval Museum where the imperial boats of the Ottoman era are displayed. Behind the jetty, Barbaros tomb designed by Sinan and Sinan Pasha mosque, dating back to 1553, are visible. Past the State Guest House, the Çırağan Palace offers a

View of the Bosphorus.
Map of the Bosphorus.

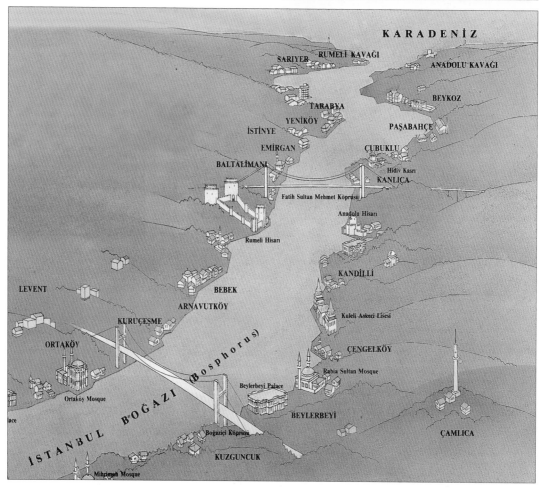

Views of "Yalı"s and Bosphorus.

magnificent view. Sultan Abdulaziz spent very little time in this palace which he ordered to be built by Serkis Balyan between the years 1863-1867, while Sultan Murad IV lived here for 28 years.

After 1909 the palace was used as Meclis-i Mebusan (Parliament) building and was destroyed by a fire on January 20, 1919. It was restored in recent years and is functioning today together with an adjoining hotel. The green background to the Çırağan Palace belongs to Yıldız Park. Here takes place the Yıldız Palace with the Şale (Chalet) Kiosk which was opened as museum and the Çadır and Malta Kiosks which

View of the Bosphorus.

At the seaside, adjoining the park, the building of the Egyptian Consulate built in Art Nouveau style can be seen. This building was dedicated to the mother of Abbas Hilmi Pasha, Governor of Egypt. A bit further there is the Bebek Mosque built by Mimar Kemalettin between the years 1910-1913. The Kavafyan House dating back to 1751 and the Bosphorus University surrounded by green scenery seem to look down at the Bebek Bay.

After Bebek, our boat steers to Rumelihisarı. Here we get face to face with the magnificent Sultan Mehmed Bridge looking like the second collier of the Bosphorus. The view of Rumelihisarı embracing the sea seems to melt into the silhouette of the bridge.

Before conquering Istanbul, Sultan Mehmet the Conqueror ordered Rumelihisarı to be built opposite to

Kanlıca Bay.

were recently restored and are being used as cafés.

After the Çırağan Palace, the Ortaköy Mosque can be seen with its lean minarettes and exquisite craftmanship. Passing this mosque which Sultan Abdülmecit ordered to be built by Karabet Balyan in 1854 in Baroque style, we see the wooden "yalı"s which Sultan Abdülhamid II gave to his daughters and they sail under the bridge, a 20th century symbol.

The bridge which connects Europe and Asia is 1074 m long and was opened to traffic in 1973. Then comes Kuruçeşme. Here, we see the Galatasaray lsland, covering a 2499 sq.m. area. The few remaining castles in the midst of green gardens offer an unique view.

Arnavutköy's architecture of adjoining buildings is different from the rest. Then we come to the pearl of the Bosphorus, the Bebek Bay. With its yachts, houses and green hinterland, Bebek is the most elegant district of lstanbul.

Beautiful view of Bosphorus.

Anadoluhisarı in 1452 to safeguard the Bosphorus. The big tower next to the door was built by Sadrazam Çandarlı Halil Pasha, the towers to the north by vizier Saruca Pasha, and the tower to the south by Zaganos Pasha. This magnificent monument was finished in 4 months prior to the conquering of Istanbul.

The building on top of the Hisar surrounded by parks belonged to the famous Turkish poet Tevfik Fikret and today is referred to as Aşiyan Museum. Sailing to Baltalimanı, we see a building used as hospital today which was built by the order of Büyük Reşit Pasha and given to Princess Fatma as gift.

After Baltalimanı, we reach Emirgan. We see the Şerifler Yalısı, which was built in 1635 by Şerif Abdülillah Pasha. This "yalı" was originally intended as summerhouse and the part remaining to be seen today is the men's castle. The green hills belonging to Emirgan Park, some historical castles in this park have been restored and are now being used for touristic purposes.

After Emirgan with lots of green parks our ferry passes a bay in İstinye and reaches Yeniköy where shores are adorned by "yalı"s. The Afif Pasha Yalısı is striking with its exquisite craftsmanship. One "yalı" built in Yeniköy by Abbas Halim Pasha, Governor of Egypt

in the 19th century is known by the name of his brother Sadrazam Sait Halim Pasha. On the other side of the jetty we can see the Faik and Bekir Beyler yalı's, the Kalkavanlar Yalısı and many others. The Italian Consulate is also an interesting architectural building.

Past Yeniköy and sailing towards Tarabya, the view is enhanced by the Kalender Orduevi (army-house), Huber Pasha Yalısı and Tarabya Grand Hotel. In Büyükdere, one of the yalı's was bought by the Koç family and converted into the Sadberk

"Yalı"s at Yeniköy.

121

View of the Fatih Sultan Mehmed Bridge from Rumeli Hisar.
Beylerbeyi Shore.

Hanım Museum. Today the archaeology and ethnography sections of this museum are noteworthy. Sarıyer and Rumelikavağı are known for their cheap and fresh fish restaurants. Opposite Rumelikavağı takes place Anadolukavağı. The boat stays here for two hours.

After eating fish at Rumelikavağı, the sightseeing continues at the other side of the Bosphorus. First we view the Beykoz Pavilion. This pavilion amidst a green park was built by Mehmet Ali Kavalalı, Governor of Egypt and given as a gift to Sultan

Abdulmecit in 1854. Then we steer to Paşabahçe where the Bottle, Glass and Rakı factories are situated and pass Çubuklu where on top of a hill we see the Kuleli building and the Hidiv Pavilion.

Being built by Abbas Hilmi Pasha, Khedive of Egypt this castle has been restored in recent years and now is used for touristic purposes. After Çubuklu we pass the poetic Kanlıca bay and arrive in Anadoluhisarı. This Hisar (castle) was built in 1395 by Yıldırım Beyazıt.

The oldest yalı between Kanlıca-Anadoluhisarı is the Amcazade Hüseyin

Tarabya Bay.
Anadoluhisar.

near the Küçüksu Stream displays an exquisite stone craftmanship. It was ordered to be built as a three-storey building by Sultan Abdülmecit in 1856. The interior part is decorated with elegant pencil drawings. The graceful fountain in front of the pavilion, built in Ampiric style, was dedicated to Sultan Selim III's mother Princess Mihrişah in 1806.

When our boat reaches Kandilli, we see the Count Ostrorog Yalısı with a background of green forest. This red-painted yalı with plenty of windows was built by a Polish count. The count arrived in Istanbul in 1900 and became a legal adviser to the Ottoman Empire. Next to this yalı is the Mehmet Emin Pasha Yalısı, which has a long frontage towards the sea and was built by Mehmet Emin Pasha who became Governor of Aleppo in 1850 and later a Grand-Vizier. Between Kandilli and Çengelköy, we see the Kuleli Askeri Lisesi (Military School) a stone building with long frontage, dating back to 1863.

A bit further to the jetty in Çengelköy we can see the red vaccine painted Sadullah

Some boats on the Bosphorus.
Afif Paşa Yalı.

Pasha Yalısı. From this red vaccine painted yalı dating back to 1699, there remains only the Divan house today. The ceiling plated with gold and flower panel-covered walls are very interesting. They were restored recently. Another Yalı in Kanlıca is the Etem Pert Yalısı, a wooden embroidery which stood up to the year by preserving its original outlook. Still another striking yalı is the red painted Hekimbaşı Salih Efendi Yalısı between Kanlıca and Anadolu Hisarı. This Yalı consists of one-floor, two-floor and three-floor premises and was built by Sultan Abdülmecit's Chief Physician Salih Efendi in 1848.

Sailing past Hisar, the Küçüksu Pavilion

View of the Bosphorus from Beylerbeyi.

Pasha Yalısı. Built in the 18th century, this building passed from hand to hand until it was acquired by Sadullah Pasha in 19th century and became. known under his name.

The original drawings in the oval room of this two storey building are striking. When our boat comes to the vicinity of Beylerbeyi Jetty, we can see next to the jetty the mosque built by Sultan Abdülhamid 1 for his mother Princess Rabia in 1778.

Then we are face to face with the magnificence of Beylerbeyi Palace which contrasts with the Bosphorus bridge. It was built as a summer palace by architect Serkis Balyan upon the order of Sultan Abdülaziz between the years 1861-1865. It has three floors consisting of men's (selamlık) and women's (harem) divisions.

The furniture is an example of that time. In the upper part of the wide garden are three kiosks known as Yellow, Marble and Stable kiosks. Past Beylerbeyi the Fethi Ahmet Pasha Yalısı in Kuzguncuk known as "Pink Yalı" was built in the 18th century.

In Üsküdar we see a mosque built by Architect Sinan for Kanuni Sultan Süleyman's daughter Princess Mihrimah at the jetty place that dates back to 1548 and at the shore there is the Şemsi Pasha Mosque built by the same architect in 1580.

Not far from here is the Kız Kulesi (Maiden's Tower), one of the symbols of Istanbul. The tower was erected on rocks at 180 m distance to the shore in 1718 after the Byzantine original collapsed. We now finish our trip between the historical monuments of the most beautiful passage in the world. This tour amongst nature and history will provide you unforgettable memories.

Sadberk Hanım Museum.

DEFTERDAR
151

HASKÖY

KULAKSIZ

Sütlüce Vapur İsk.
5 Mayıs Parkı
KUMBARACI CAD.

AYVANSARAY
BALIKHANE

Ayvansaray Vapur İsk.

Hasköy Vapur İsk.

116

Kulaksız Mezarlığı

ÇEVRE YOLU

Camiş S.

Aksemsettin Parkı

BALAT

Balat Vapur İsk.

TEPEBAŞI
96
213
49
32

H   A   L

(GOLDEN

Kasımpaşa Vapur İsk.

KASIMPAŞA

ŞİŞHANE

TÜNEL
94
192
195
155
177

NEKAPI CAD.

İRNEKAPI
133

106   157

DRAMAN

FENER

Fener Vapur İsk.

KARAGÜMRÜK

158   153

142

CARŞAMBA

Haliç Parkı

Halıç Parkı

ATATÜRK KÖPRÜSÜ

125
124

İ

HORN)

6

GALATA KÖPRÜSÜ

Metro
Ulubatlı Hasan İst.

193

Metro

ZEYREK
208

KÜÇÜKPAZAR

EMİNÖ
139
148
221

SİRK

15

129 FATİH

SÜLEYMANİYE
182

SARAÇHANE
186
175
144

162

143
181

ÇAPA

ÇINDRESI
112
17

95

72

ADNAN   MENDERES   BULVARI

Metro
Aksaray İst.

 ATATÜRK

202

Darülaceze Cad.

80

BEYAZIT
179
222

P

EMİNÖ

FINDIKZADE

MILLET   CADDESI

AKSARAY
14

P

ORDU   CADDESI

YENİÇERİLER   CADDESI

KAPALI ÇARŞI

12
128

NURUOSMANİYE CAD.

SULTA

ALTIMERMER

HASEKI

INKILAP CAD.

79
87

MESIH
66

NİŞANCA

DIVAN   YOLU

233

HEKIMOĞLU

CERRAHPAŞA

Langa bostanları S.
21

HAVUZ KEMAL CAD.

HAVUZ TÜCCAR

KÜBELI CAD.

MULLA S.

YENİKAPI

SAMIL

YOLU

KENNEDY

CADDESI

Yenikapı
Deniz Otobüsü İsk.

KUMKAPI
13

A. Nafiz GURMAN

MARMARA   DENİZİ
(SEA OF MARMARA)

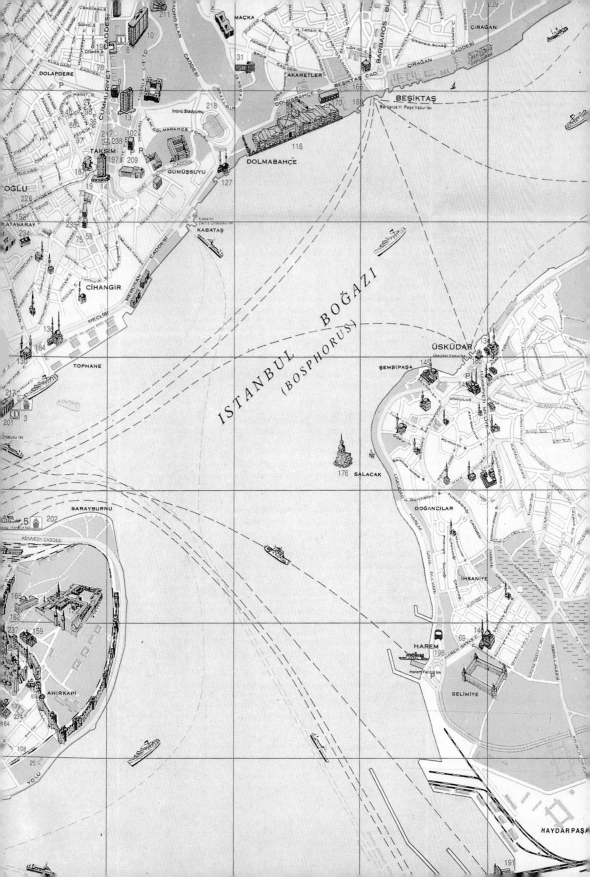

PUBLICATIONS LIST

- **TURKEY (LITTLE FORMAT)**
  (In English, German, French)

- **TOURISTIC GUIDE OF TURKEY**
  (In English, French, German, Japanese, Turkish)

- **TREASURES OF TRUKEY (LARGE FORMAT)**
  (In English, French, German, Italian, Spanish)

- **THE CITY OF TWO CONTINENTS, ISTANBUL**
  (In English, French, German, Italian, Spanish)

- **TREASURES OF ISTANBUL (LARGE FORMAT)**
  (In English, French, German)

- **THE TOPKAPI PALACE (LITTLE FORMAT)**
  (In English, French, German, Italian, Spanish, Japanese)

- **THE TOPKAPI PALACE (LARGE FORMAT)**
  (In English, French, German)

- **PAMUKKALE - HIERAPOLIS**
  (In English, French, German, Italian, Spanish, Swedish, Dutch)

- **CAPPADOCIA**
  (In English, French, German, Italian, Spanish)

- **EPHESUS, KUŞADASI, PRIENE, MILET, DIDYMA**
  (In English, French, German)

- **MARMARIS - BODRUM**
  (In English, French, German)

- **GUIDE TO EASTERN TURKEY**
  (In English, French, German)

- **THE CRYSTAL - CLEAR WATERS OF THE TURQUOISE COAST - THE BLUE VOYAGE**
  (In English)

- **ANTALYA**
  (In English, French, German, Italian)

- **MEVLANA AND THE MEVLANA MUSEUM**
  (In English, French, German)

- **THE EVOLUTION OF TURKISH ART AND ARCHITECTURE** (In English)

- **CHORA**
  (In English, French, German)

- **TURKISH CARPET ART**
  (In English, French, German)

- **THE BLUE SAILING (LARGE FORMAT)**
  (In English)

- **ISTANBUL (LITTLE FORMAT)**
  (In English, French, German)

İLHAN AKŞİT

İlhan Akşit was born in Denizli in 1940. He graduated as an archaeologist in 1965. When he was assigned to a post related to the excavation of Aphrodisias. He was director of the Çanakkale - Troy Museum between 1968-1976, during which time the replica of the Trojan horse we now see on the site was constructed. He directed the excavation of the Chryse Apollo temple over a period of five years. From 1976-1978, the author acted as director of the Underwater Archaeology Museum, Bodrum and was appointed Director of National Palaces in 1978. During his directorship, the author was responsible for the restoration and reopeninig of these palaces to the public after an extended period of closure. In 1982 the retired from his post to take up a career as an author of popular books on Turkish archaeology and tourism. He has nearly 3 titles to his credit to date, including 'The Story of Troy', 'The Civilizatons of Anatolia', 'The Blue Journey', 'Istanbul', and The Hititites'.